Get the whole collection

SHAKING THE TREE

V|5

BRAZEN. SHORT. MEMOIR.

but I'm still here

Memoir Writers Press is an imprint of IMWA
3639 Midway Drive, Ste. B-198
San Diego, CA 92110-5254
InternationalMemoirWriters.org

This book is a memoir anthology. It reflects the authors' present
recollections of experiences over time. Some names and characteristics
have been changed, some events may have been compressed,
and dialogue may be recreated.

Copyedited by Erin Willar
Proofread by Tracy J. Jones
Book cover and interior design by Monkey C Media

First Edition

ISBN: 978-1-959793-00-7 (trade paperback)
ISBN: 978-1-959793-01-4 (ebook)

Library of Congress Control Number: available upon request

Dedicated to Suzanne Spector
and everyone who dares to love with "Dancing Hearts Emojis."

Dear Reader,

You know that feeling when you get knocked to the ground and don't want to get up again? But then somehow, someway, you find your way to unsteady feet, look around, and start walking again. That's the feeling we have captured in these pages. Our hope is that when you feel like this, you can open to any story, read it, and be infused with the strength to take that first unsteady step. We hope these bold writers inspire you; writing the brazen truth is not always easy. But they did—and they are still here.

Happy reading,

Marni and Tracy

CONTENTS

RIM TO RIM

LINDSEY SALATKA

Halfway down the Grand Canyon, we noticed the HUGE SIGNS posted on the side of the trail:

ARE YOU FIT AND ADVENTUROUS?
YOU FIT THE PROFILE OF 3 RECENT DEATHS
AND ENDLESS INJURIES.
PROCEED WITH CAUTION!
NO RESCUE CREW WILL BE SENT FOR YOU!

Were these signs directed at me? Maybe, but it was too late to turn back.

Four months earlier, my brother had presented the idea. "They call it Rim to Rim. You hike down the south side of the canyon and back up the north on the same day. We're going to do it with Billy and his wife and their friends; they've said it's great. Want to join?"

"Sounds fantastic," I said, before the question was even out of his mouth. "We're in!" I added, before I had checked with my husband. I didn't ask a single follow-up question. Not "How many miles is that exactly?" Not "Do I need any equipment?" Not "Should I be extremely or even somewhat fit?" I'd been to the Grand Canyon before, and I knew my brother—he was no Grizzly Adams. Plus, I'd met Billy and his wife; it was doubtful they were hitting the StairMaster in their downtime. I would be in the company of people just like me—what could possibly go wrong?

1

For the next four months, I rarely thought about the Rim to Rim trip. I certainly didn't step up my sporadic exercise routine. I remember briefly thinking about footwear. I didn't own hiking boots and wasn't crazy about buying something I wouldn't wear again. Besides, I knew one thing: it was a bad idea to wear new shoes on any adventure; things could go sideways as you simultaneously admire and curse your shiny purchase. Borrowing trail shoes was much wiser, and I was pretty sure my stepmom had a pair. Her feet were only slightly smaller than mine, certainly not enough to matter.

I didn't ask how far the Rim to Rim trip was until the night before, when I received a variety of vague answers, so I stepped into that giant crack in the earth with assumptions based on my previous experience—it would be about eight miles down, a half-mile across, and a matching eight up the other side. Yes, that's far and perhaps warrants preparation. But the hike down? Who prepares to walk down a hill, and how would one even do that? And the crossing part? That's like a flat stroll around the block. I was a bit worried about the eight miles up. *That might sting*, I thought.

The night before, we drove up from Sedona through Flagstaff and stopped at Babbitt's. They had a sale on hiking sticks. So, of course, I bought one, not for a second questioning why it was a good idea to drop cash on a stick I'd never use again but not on shoes. I also bought a pair of zip-off pants because my brother told me our hike would start at a brisk 4 a.m., which I assumed was so we could finish by lunchtime.

When we arrived at the South Rim, we checked into our hotel and joined the rest of our hiking crew around a campfire. Billy and his friends passed around a bottle of tequila, taking long slugs. I was smart enough to turn this down, but it furthered my assumption that this big ole hike was not a big ole deal.

Six hours later, at 3:55 a.m., I stood at the top of Bright Angel Trail, wearing a T-shirt, sweatshirt, my stepmom's slightly too-small shoes, my sparkly new zip-off pants, and a backpack that held a flashlight, a bottle of water, and a bag of my favorite trail-mix—a 50–50 blend of nuts and M&Ms, which I figured would be more than adequate, given that I had just eaten a PowerBar. I could see my breath. The tequila drinkers were wearing headlamps over bandanas, joking around while stretching in the pitch black.

"Are we ready?" they hollered, at four on the dot.

"Ready as we'll ever be!" I scrambled to pull out my flashlight, praying the batteries weren't dead.

The Tequila Crew took off running. My foursome stood briefly staring at each other, and then we blindly tripped into one of the seven wonders of the natural world. Hiking in complete darkness on a skinny, rocky trail beside a steep canyon seemed risky. I thought about suggesting we wait until there was more light, but what did I know? Moreover, this was no time to start being sensible. We hoped to eventually catch (and maybe pass!) the tequila crew. My toes started aching pretty quickly, followed by my knees, but I didn't want to break the complaint seal. I was not the weak link! I could do hard things!

About three hours in, we stopped at a pull-off area to remove our sweatshirts and drink some water. I had not seen one place to refill our bottles, and mine was half empty. Then, in the burgeoning light, we noticed the aforementioned warning signs. Everything started to feel less fun. Could this be a bad idea? No, I could do this. I might lose some toenails, but I'd make it out. No complaining!

Four hours in, we arrived at the bottom. *Almost halfway there!* I thought. We stopped at the river, cool and beautiful, but didn't stay long, because we were starving. The Native American trading post at Phantom Ranch was low on supplies, but I bought a stale bagel sandwich and a bottle of water. I also bought a bag of straight M&Ms because who was I trying to fool? I could feel my heartbeat in my toes, and the nuts? They were just placeholders.

We crossed to the other side of the river on a scenic bridge that held breathtaking views. But before we could begin the ascent, we needed to cross "the box." I hadn't anticipated anything about the damn box. Not the lack of shade or breeze, not the four-mile slog to reach the trail out (three-and-a-half miles more than my estimate), and certainly not the 107-degree heat that blasted us as we stepped away from the river.

Halfway through the box, I demolished the complaint seal like an ice pick through frosting. "I think my kneecaps are going to pop off."

"I jacked up my ankle jumping from that giant rock," my brother said.

"My hips keep popping," my sister-in-law chimed in.

"My face is melting off," my husband added.

Something felt so good about calling out my pain, hearing the response of my fellow hikers, and knowing I wasn't alone in my misery. The four of us shared a weak laugh but then reverted to silence. We had only completed the easy half of an excruciating journey—we needed to ration what energy we had left.

It was then I looked up. Really took in the trail looming ahead of me. My legs began shaking, my stomach churned, my toes were on fire, and I heard a ringing in my ears.

It was steep.

It was slippery.

It was covered in loose rock.

Terror struck.

I can't do this, I thought. I can't make it ten more feet, let alone to the top.

Falling, injuring myself, is inevitable.

I am officially an idiot. I am an idiot who deserves to die down here because I'm impulsive and, I don't think things through, and

THEY POST SIGNS ABOUT PEOPLE LIKE ME.

I was delivered from my self-loathing trance by the sound of my husband's voice.

"Come on, let's get out of this hole."

I nodded, found a spot of hard-packed dirt, planted my stick, and pulled myself onward and upward.

At about 4 p.m., twelve hours into our big day, I called out to people heading toward us, "Excuse me, how far are we from the top?"

There had been water fountains on this trail but not many, and the M&Ms had been decimated hours earlier. It felt like every turn was going to bring a view of the finish line, but no. Interestingly, no two answers were the same. "Two more turns!" "Fifteen minutes!" "About another 1.5 hours," one guy said.

I hated that guy.

4

I was salty in both attitude and skin texture, but it turned out, he was the most accurate. Fourteen hours and twenty-four miles after our first step, we straggled out to find the tequila crew freshly showered, laughing, and imbibing. They would cross back the next day in a feat called Rim-to-Rim-to-Rim.

I could barely move, let alone laugh or imbibe. My back spasmed for hours when I lay down for the night in my hotel bed.

After this outing, one might assume I've become more thoughtful in my decision-making, less impulsive, that I conduct research before saying yes to things.

But I don't.

My pattern of underthinking continues, and while sometimes I'm convinced it's because I'm a Grand Canyon-sized idiot, I am also learning empathy for myself, because I've come to understand why I am this way. For me, overthinking leads to anxiety, fear, self-doubt, and sometimes paralysis. And I want to spend as little time as possible in those states of mind.

However, I also know that there will be times when anxiety, fear, and self-doubt will be inevitable: Friends will have their hearts broken, my children will struggle, people I love will die. I cannot stop these things from happening.

What I can do is choose to stay light and nimble while I can, to laugh and participate in the absurdities of life every chance I get, and to say yes to adventures with a joyful heart, even if that's a fourteen-hour hike to what might feel like the molten center of the earth.

When it comes to that kind of adventure, you can count on me to underthink—and go all in—Rim to Rim.

BROKEN TARMAC

PAUL STEINKOENIG

"Jalalabad is on fire!" yelled the guy sitting next to me. We were about twenty minutes into the packed and bumpy flight. The pre-departure report had indicated big trouble brewing in Jalalabad. It wasn't like I hadn't been warned. My nerves were already jumpy. I felt like I was sitting on a pile of ants and could hardly remain seated. The plane's condition didn't help, as it reeked of disrepair.

It was 2005 and my first day as a public outreach officer with the United Nations. Our hope was to bring free and fair elections to Afghanistan. As a volunteer, I was proud to be one of a handful of Americans to participate. We had the goal of taking a country in the middle of too many years of battle and chaos and helping it start a new government of its own choosing. The whole world was watching. Unfortunately, a recent rash of roadside bombings and violent shootings jeopardized the election. The day before, a woman working with one of the small aid agencies had been kidnapped just outside of Kabul. The shit was real.

"The airport is burning! It's closed! There's no way we will get out of this plane in Jalalabad!" yelled my seatmate. He kept checking the messages on his cell phone. Since I did not yet have my Afghanistan phone, I depended on others to share the updates. My heart thudded heavily in my chest like a bass drum; we were literally flying into the fire.

***

That morning, we had been pulled into an urgent team briefing in Kabul right before we left for the airport. A no-nonsense UN compound chief of staff paced before us. His former military career showed clearly in his posture. His gray hair and tone of voice bristled. "Good morning, everyone. So, earlier today, *Newsweek* broke a story about an American soldier guarding the prisoners at Guantanamo Bay. The soldier tore apart a Koran in front of one of the Afghan prisoners. Then, well, he supposedly flushed the Koran down the toilet." People around the room gasped. My gut clenched. I exchanged worried glances with the man standing next to me. News like this could start a war. The chief of staff continued. "At this moment, Jalalabad has erupted in violence."

And yet, an hour later, we headed for the airport to get started on the elections. I would be working in the eastern region. From day one of my arrival in Afghanistan, the pressure to get busy had been intense: every day wasted was a loss to the number of people reached about the upcoming vote. The eastern provinces were behind and needed help getting up and running. There was no time to waste.

***

Forty-five minutes into the ninety-minute flight to Jalalabad, and my head was spinning. From what we gathered, the *Newsweek* article had ignited a grenade, unleashing a torrent of anti-US mobs who were shooting guns in the street, breaking windows, and setting things on fire while they chanted, "Death to America!" And yet, even in the face of all that, there was a flutter of hope in my chest for my mission—free and fair elections in Afghanistan. As a public outreach officer, I would be pulling together a team of locals to train the larger population on the essentials of holding an election.

In rural Afghanistan, where democratic elections were new, we had many miles to walk before voting could begin. There were no polling places. People did not have IDs. And some of the local people were determined to stop the election. Not everyone wanted a democracy. The week before, a young Afghan boy had flagged down a car of international aid workers, wanting to sell them some chocolate. They slowed, stopped, and opened their window. The boy threw a grenade into the car, killing three. A vice-like headache took hold.

***

I had left behind a private psychotherapy practice in New Mexico after years of feeling achy, restless, and stuck. I'd had a gnawing fear that life wasn't just passing me by but that I had actually stopped living it. Months flew by with me on autopilot.

A friend of mine had visited Afghanistan years before. His tales ignited my curiosity and passion to see that magical place for myself. At night, I would read stories or watch the news about Afghanistan, and I could feel an actual pull toward the struggling people of that faraway country. It brought back memories of having been raised by a father who beat me regularly and a depressed mother who sometimes starved me for food. I knew what it was like to have no voice—to need someone, anyone to extend a hand. When 9/11 hit, I knew I could not sit still. I wanted to be one of those hands for the Afghan people.

***

As our flight grew closer to Jalalabad, conflicting gossip spread among the passengers.

There's an angry mob at the airport.

The airport is calm; no violent incidents were reported.

A bomb just went off right by a plane.

The plane bucked as we hit the uneven runway. Through the small window, I saw smoke from the burning buildings filling the sky. I was a mix of emotions. *Do I even want to get off the plane? What will meet us on the other side of those doors?* As the plane came to a stop, the pilot announced through tinny speakers, "We're very sorry, but all passengers must return to Kabul. We're only briefly landing the plane to allow an additional passenger to board." My seatmates all glanced at one another. A collective sigh of relief escaped many lips. Looking around the plane itself, we wondered where this new person would sit. The flight was completely full. Then the tinny voice returned, "Attention, passengers. We need your assistance. The head of the UN Afghanistan project needs a ride back to Kabul; is anyone willing to give up their seat?"

I couldn't understand what they were asking. It was too dangerous to get off the plane, yet they wanted one person to give up their seat for the big boss. That one person would remain in Jalalabad. They said the big boss was needed urgently at headquarters. My body struggled to catch up with my racing thoughts. I was on information overload. Suddenly, with startling clarity, a beam of light pierced my heart. I had wanted to stop living my life on autopilot. I had wanted to grow and be of service. *Here was such an opportunity, but I am really thinking about raising my hand and volunteering to get off the plane?* As I debated—all in the space between two heartbeats— I was raising my hand.

"I'll give up my seat!"

The whole plane froze in silence. The captain looked surprised, as if he couldn't believe anyone would volunteer. My seatmate was the first to speak. "Way to go, dude! Good luck." I stood up, made my way down the aisle, and got off the plane.

When my feet landed on the tarmac, the pilot threw my two small bags out of the airplane's door. I looked around. The city was on fire. Plumes of thick gray smoke surrounded me. I could see the flames of two small buildings just outside the airport on my right. As I took in the crumpled gray war-torn tarmac, dust and grit filled my eyes.

The pilot kept the engines running. With the twin propellers roaring near me, the blowback whipped the air into a frenzy. Everything seemed disjointed and loud. *Now I've done it. There's no turning back.* I felt lost, wishing someone would take me by the arm and show me what to do. I wanted a welcome wagon to cheer my brave decision. But I was alone.

Then, as if out of nowhere, I noticed an upscale sparkling-white SUV idling nearby. *Maybe that car is for me.* The door opened to reveal Peter Erban, the head of the UN Afghanistan electoral program. As he boarded the plane, he shouted over his shoulder, "Nice to meet you! Thanks for giving up your seat."

I turned to make my way to the SUV—my ride off that tarmac—and to the safety of the UN compound when the car suddenly sped away. I watched in shock as the SUV pulled away in one direction and the plane taxied off in another. The diminishing roar of the aircraft allowed new sounds to come through from the riot-filled city.

Rat-a-tat of machine guns to my right.

Jarring booms as buildings exploded to my left.

And that smell: the stench of burning rubber overwhelmed my senses.

Smoke and dust assaulted me from all directions.

I was in the middle of a war scene.

***

What the hell was I thinking, volunteering to get off the plane? I stood there in shock. The readiness and certainty I had felt just a few moments ago now seemed like a distant memory. Death felt closer than ever. I knew on a visceral level that at any minute, shooters could come charging at me and that I might be kidnapped and held for ransom—or worse.

My stomach jumped and twisted every time a bomb went off.

And then, for reasons I don't think I will ever understand, a sense of calm washed over me. I felt as if I were standing in a place where everything was unreal and playing out in slow motion, like I was watching a movie scene unfold frame by frame.

I was both jittery and prepared to take on anything life had to throw at me. Autopilot mode was gone. Something bigger than myself had my attention.

THE PINK DRESS

CHAU PHAM

I can't believe I'm going to the school dance. It's seventh grade, school's almost done, and the hallways are lined with posters that read "School Dance, Friday the 7th, Be There or Be Square!" And Dad said I could go. He was leafing through letters when he said yes—without looking directly at me. He had just come home from work in his white shirt and skinny black tie, and he smelled like Old Spice. Usually, when I looked up at him, I always felt so small, but now, in this moment, I felt like I was being pulled up into the atmosphere.

Two months ago, when I asked, then begged, if I could go to a Billy Joel concert, he screamed "No!" and told me that if I went to the concert, it would be "a symbol of shame on our family." *What does that even mean?* Dad didn't understand. Billy Joel is my absolute favorite singer. I stare at his cassette tape all the time—Billy, all in black and white, sitting on the bed, staring down at a theater mask. God, he is the coolest older-man piano-playing pop star I have ever seen. I know every single word to every single song from every single album. I knew Dad wouldn't change his mind, so I sat on my bed and cried.

We came to this country twelve years ago from Vietnam, and Dad has been busy learning English, working a nine-to-five job at the church's office, supporting seven children, and putting food on the table and gas in the car on an immigrant's salary. I'm a twelve-year-old foreign girl in a small town in Upstate New York. We've invaded small-town America by living right next door, the only Asian family for fifty miles. When I look around, I feel as if I am drowning in a "perfectly trimmed grass lawn, two cars in the driveway, taking the family up to the lake on the weekends" kind of America. Our front lawn looks like a jungle, with rose bushes next to tropical plants next to tall, browning evergreen trees. One of our garages has been converted into a bedroom because seven girls ages eight to twenty will not fit into a three-bed-room house, no matter how hard you try. It was either build more bedrooms or be murdered by all the clothes, makeup, and "I had it first" drama.

If I'm going to the dance, I'm gonna need a dress. I dive into the clothes hanging in my closet. I look in my half of the closet at all my shirts and dresses. Nothing. Then I look through the other half at the clothes that are not mine. I'm not allowed to touch them, but I don't care. This dress has to be special. The whole school is going to be there.

Panic rises up. I have nothing to wear. There's no way I can buy anything; I don't have any money. *Good God, what do I do now?* I run downstairs to my older sister's room. She is lying on her bed, reading a book for English. My older sister is in high school, and she is so much cooler and smarter than me. If I tell her my problem, she'll know what to do.

And she does. She's the middle child, the fourth. The peacemaker. All she wants is for everyone to get along, and she'll even sacrifice herself to make that happen. She's soft and open-minded in the face of our controlling older sisters. They trample on her because they know they can.

She listens to me tenderly and then creases her eyebrows in a compassionate glance.

"I'll make you a dress for the dance. I can use other dresses I have. I'll make something pretty for you."

I am taken aback by her kindness, but also I worry, "How long is it gonna take? The dance is on Friday."

"I can do it," she says confidently.

Every day, I'm like a kid at Christmastime, waiting for toys to appear under the tree. I rush home from school to find my sister at the dining table, cutting up her pretty pink dresses and sewing them together by the dim light of the chandelier. When it grows late into the night, she moves everything into her room, sits on the edge of her bed,

12

and continues to sew together the pieces of lace and satin by hand. On the third night, after she has cut and sewn for hours, I fall asleep on her bed. She wakes me up and tells me to go up to my own bed. The fourth night arrives, and it's nearly midnight. I've fallen asleep again as she is sewing the bottom of my dress while it's on a hanger on top of the doorframe. I lift my head up and ask, "Is it done yet?"

She smiles and keeps on sewing. "Almost."

On the fifth day, I rush home from school. I'm as light as a feather because nothing is going to stop me today. My dad said yes, and my sister made me a dress. I hurry downstairs to my sister's room, where the door is open, and the room is dark. She isn't home; she's already left to go to her part-time job at the local diner. On the open door, on a hanger over the top, is the pink dress. It's lacy and high-collared, with long sleeves, and the bottom half is full and shiny, made of pure pink satin. My sister used the top half of her junior prom dress and attached it to the bottom half of another dress, and raised it on the side so it would fit me. I have never seen anything so beautifully unique in my whole life. It is so pink and so pretty, and so special because she'd worn it before and I knew how beautiful she looked in it. I try it on, and I feel like a queen. It's magic, and suddenly, I belong in that neighborhood, at the school dance, and in this world.

I arrive at school, float into the gym, and I dance. I drink punch, and I stand proudly in my dress. Girls tell me how gorgeous I look. They are in awe and think it's incredibly expensive, and I must have gotten it from the fanciest, farthest-away country.

When I get home, my sister is there, changing out of her waitress uniform. Her hair is in a tight bun, and her brown-and-cream uniform smells like fried oil. She smiles at me and asks, "Well, what do you think?" I tell her I love it and that it's so beautiful. I twirl in it, and she laughs.

***

I hold my sister's hand as she lays in bed; this time, I'm in a hospital. A severe stroke has left her in a coma. I wouldn't know it for three weeks, but she would wake up paralyzed on one-half of her body, with permanent damage to her short-term and working memory. Her long-term memory, her speech, and her executive functioning would be severely disrupted, but she would live. And I would hear her laugh again.

"Hi," I say, thinking about the pink dress hanging on the door. "I'm still here," I say.

SKATEAWAY

HANNAH ANDREWS

Tucson, Arizona
March 1995

Looking back, it's surreal. I can almost hear the crackle of old videotape as the memory replays, like a movie or some retro television series. The motel signpost is familiar but blurry. It reads SuperSix or maybe EconoEight, some mishmash name, like two cheap motels hooked up and this was their ugly baby. We checked into a room that reeked of Lysol-doused ghosts of cigarettes past; its balding orangish carpet was full of mystery stains.

Fate had dropped it, off center, onto a giant parking lot, then us at its doorstep. It was the opposite of opulent, nearing oppressive, but it was cheap and safe. Plus, the parking lot was always deserted and smooth as black ice—perfect for rollerblading, a free workout for two gym rats on a budget. Steve and I were twenty-six years old and less than a year into marriage. Legally bound and determined to escape the dreary, redundantly inclement Midwest, where dreams went to die.

"I refuse to spend half my waking existence warming my engine or scraping ice off the windshield of life," angsty me had whined one sub-zero Chicago morning.

"Tucson?" He'd smiled and, seeing joy flush my face, added, "I'm your Huckleberry."

Indeed, he was. One line from a Val Kilmer movie and my bags were packed.

I'd developed a taste for the Southwest as a child. My extended family would caravan cross-country to visit relatives in Phoenix and escape the gray midwestern winters. A colorful *Arizona Highways* calendar hung like hope in our midwestern kitchen. Saguaro cacti waved prickly arms to me from that painted desert.

Steve and I homed in on Phoenix's southern cousin. Tucson was smaller and quirkier and boasted 350-plus days of sunshine. I would stop sliding into my seasonal funks. Between the sunshine and soulmate Steve, I'd always be smiling.

Arizona promised some sort of magic, or maybe just a different sort of ordinary. Throw in one of those cute little tile-roofed adobe houses, and my fairy tale would be complete.

"Cardio time, babe. Love you." My hubby tossed me an air kiss, rollerbladed out the door, and disappeared into our new southwestern scenery. I'd opted out, immersed in a midday *X-Files* marathon and silently battling nicotine addiction. I was on day three of quitting smoking.

Steve hated smoking. I absolutely adored it, but I adored him more. Steve had said, "Babe, it only takes three days and determination to break any addiction. Sugar will quell any nicotine fits."

I smush-stretched a taffy-like Silly Putty, cajoled it into a cylindrical shape, drew it to my mouth, and took a deep, introspective drag. I thought about our trek to Tucson and the path I'd been denied.

Steve had been in such a rush to get there, he couldn't be bothered with diversions. I'd wanted to putter across Route 66, the historic Mother Road that ran semi-parallel to us most of the trip. Road signs at connecting crossroads had beckoned me, whisper-shouting, "You're on the wrong road!" I'd highlighted our giant Rand McNally Road Atlas with my desired deviation and even played Depeche Mode's "Route 66" ad nauseam. No dice. Steve stuck to the interstate. He wouldn't even detour to that crazy Cadillac Ranch art installment outside of Amarillo.

"Babe, it's just a bunch of cars stuck ass-up in the ground."

"It's a giant fucking metaphor, Steven, and it's almost right on the way."

Just a silly spat, I'd thought. And in the end, we'd arrived in record time, thanks to Steve.

I dug through a suitcase and pulled out our wedding photos, and my stale surroundings squiggle-dissolved away like a *Wayne's World* scene, transporting me back eight months to that deserted playground and an impulsive dare that changed everything.

I stood under the monkey bars, looked him square in the eyes, and boasted,

"I was the undisputed chicken fight champion of third grade. I beat all the big boys."

Challenge accepted—we squared off on opposite ends. I had to vertical jump to grab on, whereas he simply tip-toed and stretched a little, then bent his knees in. We hang-walked to the middle, and the battle commenced. I quickly captured him with my legs. He writhed in fake agony, then wriggled free and captured me. I caught my breath, giggled, "uncle," and let go. My hands caught his shoulders as I fell into him, and we hung there, entwined, the world revolving around us while we kissed. It felt like the beginning of forever.

One week later—same playground—marriage proposal. It didn't seem fast. It seemed completely logical to marry my best friend. Anxious for our "happily ever after" to begin as soon as possible, we eloped to Vegas.

"Stevie, baby, look! A drive-thru chapel. Ooh, Michael Jordan got married here! That's gotta be good luck." I was all in. I'd have sworn it was his breath in my lungs, that I'd have suffocated, drowned inside myself without him. Our smiles beamed through silly "Just Married" photos. We were tanned and toned in matching cutoffs and T-shirts, perched out the sunroof of my '94 Buick Regal—the sedan I'd traded my bitchin' Camaro in for, cuz I was a grownup.

The neon crackled and dimmed, and I found myself back in the stale Tucson motel with TV's Mulder and Scully. They were busy looking for some "truth" that was supposedly "out there." It seemed symbolic.

Nah, that's just the taffy talking. I need to burn off some sugar.

I grabbed my blades and peeked out the curtain. I didn't see Steve in the parking lot, but he loved to roll the access roads and side streets. Too risky for my taste. I'd just stay in, maybe teach myself guitar.

Ugh, that guitar. Shortly after our wedding, Steve decided he no longer wanted to be an engineer.

"Babe, I'm gonna be a country music star. Check out this song I wrote."

It sounded like some sort of mis-chorded country-music haiku. Totally nonsensical.

Until that moment, his mathy analytical brain had seemed to counter my dreamer self perfectly. But he'd had an epiphany.

His plan was to teach himself guitar and then wait for stardom to come calling, just ringing the bell like some 1970s Avon lady. As I looked around the room for the guitar, I thought maybe that was a sign—or one of what was becoming a whole Vegas Neon Graveyard of signs. I'd made a real commitment, for better or worse, right? Plus, his music was improving.

And that's when I noticed it.

His guitar was gone.

So was his duffle bag.

My heart in my throat, I stomped out to the Buick, reassuring myself that all of his stuff was probably in the car. After all, *I had watched him leave with just his rollerblades.*

I opened the trunk.

Empty.

Full gut punch.

I flung open the driver's-side door. A rush of heat mixed with cold reality smacked my face.

A one-word note on the seat.

"Goodbye."

The desert sun glinted off his gold wedding band. In the spotless ashtray.

Infinity so carelessly discarded.

I drove to the closest Circle K and buzzed through the aisles like a rabid contestant on *Supermarket Sweep.* I scooped up Doritos, Ben and Jerry's, and more Laffy Taffy. I emptied my arms onto the counter and looked up in amazement as a back wall of cigarettes sprang to life.

"I'll take a pack of Marlboro Lights—no, make that Marlboro Reds," I told the cashier. I raced back to the room, barely outpacing my tears. I sat on the bed, shoveling junk food into my mouth while simultaneously sob-smoking. I wailed, half-hyperventilating, to my best friend back home. "He's gone. My life is over. And I'm stuck in this shitty motel surrounded by fucking cacti.

"Pricks everywhere!"

She simply sighed and said, "Well, he couldn't have gotten far."

***

Life is so different in the rearview mirror. Nineties-me bet her future on pretty calendars and schoolyard kisses. If I could go back, I wouldn't scold her. I'd hug her. I'd tell her to relish every wrong road. Our twenties are made for epic mistakes and misadventures. I was devastated back then, but now, I just look back and laugh, like it's a lost episode of *Friends*—"The One Where My Husband Rollerbladed Away."

LOST AND FOUND

ANASTASIA ZADEIK

I realize I've left my phone behind only three blocks from home but do not go back to retrieve it. All I can think is get away. *Get away.* But driving toward I-5, I know this directive is impossible because no matter where I go, I will still be there. A blanket of invisible fog doubling as a vise wraps around me. I worry I will explode—or implode. Suffer emotional spontaneous combustion.

Perhaps I already have.

Approaching the on-ramp, the last ten minutes replay in my head. I am standing at the kitchen counter, trimming a bouquet of days-old flowers, adding fresh ones from our garden, when my husband asks, "Are you going back outside?" as he glances to the back door. My hands had been full when I came into the house, and until he asks this seemingly innocuous question, it hasn't occurred to me the door remains open. And in an instant, I know it isn't an innocuous question. It is a passive-aggressive reproach. He isn't curious about whether I'm going back out; he is criticizing me for failing to shut the door. I am trying to bring beauty back into my world, into his world, and all he had to do was take two goddamn steps to close the door, but he would rather make me feel bad by pointing out an inadequacy, however small.

And suddenly, unexpectedly, decades of rage boil over. Hundreds of moments when I've taken care of things for him without saying a word. Underwear picked up from the floor without an "are you going to wear these again?" Dirty plates loaded from the sink into the dishwasher without an "are you done eating?" Wet towels removed from beds, floors swept of dirt brought in by his shoes, toilets cleaned of his shit, doors closed that he'd left open.

He doesn't know it took every ounce of effort to get out of bed. Wash my face. Get dressed. Make coffee. To not see the days-old bouquet as impending death in a vase, but as flowers that could be refreshed. To see the sun shining despite internal clouds filled with dangerous electrical current and crazy-loud thunder—moving closer and closer until BOOM, the storm comes, and I am done, and he is there.

And so, it is upon him my rage and despair and hopelessness falls.

A deluge of words pours out of me. I am whirling out of control but can't stop it. I cannot see reason. I cannot bring to mind all the times he *has* been there *for me*, trying to understand. I cannot summon the mornings I've lain, spooned in his arms, trying to explain what it's like inside my head. How some days, my thoughts are sparks, flying loose, setting off blazes in my head. Or worse, traps of ceaseless rumination, whirlpools of quicksand. "Neurotransmitters in an endless synaptic do-loop," I say, cloaking pain in scientific terms as if this might make it hurt less.

Too many times I've woken him in the wee hours, pacing the bedroom floor, filled with self-loathing, hitting my temple with the heel of my palm, saying, "I am an idiot," over and over.

"Stop that," he says, gently. "You're not an idiot," he says. "Come back to bed."

But not this morning. This morning, he simply says, "Are you going back outside?" And the fragile control I've been clinging to for days— no weeks, months, years—slips away.

A horn sounds behind me, and I return to myself, driving to Torrey Pines on the freeway. Swerving back into my lane, I contemplate turning the wheel toward the cement barriers lining the center divide. I recall a book in which a mother deliberately killed her sociopathic son. How she was wearing her seatbelt, and he wasn't. How she survived, and he didn't. I worry about surviving a crash and becoming an even greater burden, but rather than putting aside the idea of driving into the barriers, I consider taking my seatbelt off. I want to call my children to apologize for all I've done wrong despite wanting more than anything to parent them well. Then I remember I don't have my phone. I cannot call them, and this is good. I should not lay my troubles on them; they would be so much better off without me.

Stop, I tell myself, *stop, stop, stop*, until I arrive at the parking lot by the beach.

It is hot on the road leading up to the trails at the top of the reserve, and though usually a diligent planner, I am halfway up before it occurs to me that I have no water. Once, while hiking inland with a friend in 95-degree weather with only a water bottle apiece, we turned back, aware dehydration can kill. We later learned a young woman had died that very day on that very trail. Her companion called for help, but it was too late. By the time the paramedics arrived, she had lapsed into a coma. Her body shut down. Shutting down, going to sleep, not waking up—this makes me feel envy, which I know is not the correct emotion to feel. Something is very wrong.

This is reinforced when I see the ocean and instead of the thoughts that usually ground me—that the ocean is teeming with life, and across its great expanse there are millions of people living lives I will never know about, and that, given the enormity of this, my problems are small and surmountable—I am struck by the lack of meaning of my own existence. How little I have achieved. Despair looms dark and monolithic. For the first time, when I glance across the landscape toward the water, I imagine myself purposefully walking to the edge of the cliffs. I imagine jumping. Falling.

Which is what I alluded to when I left the house that morning. When I shouted at my husband, "Maybe you'll be lucky, and I won't come back. Maybe you'll be lucky, and I'll jump."

Right before I slammed the door. Made the decision not to go back and get my phone.

And standing there, still on the road, I think of my husband, wondering if I meant it. I think of my kids. Worry he might call them, tell them what I said. Worry I might be worrying them.

There is a cluster of men ahead, and I decide to ask if I can borrow a phone to text my husband that I'm okay, so he won't call the kids. It isn't true—that I'm okay—but I've conveyed this message hundreds of times when it is patently false. So I catch up to the men and make my request. Fear of COVID-19 contagion spreads across their masked faces. Or maybe it is a reaction to the tears streaming down mine. One of the men hands me a phone, asks, "Are you okay?"

"Yes," I say, before typing the same lie in a text. *Forgot my phone. I'm okay.*

And then I head down toward the cliffs. Toward deep-blue ocean and sky-blue sky. Rose-gold sandstone. Cacti. Flowers. Scrub. Orange and purple and white and green. Waiting for relief to hit. This is my go-to place when I am overwhelmed and need solace, or a reset. I approach the spot at the edge where I habitually stop for a moment of Zen, where I've asked my children to scatter my ashes after I'm gone. "Play 'Gabriel's Oboe' and 'What a Wonderful World,'" I say. "Recite Mary Oliver. Breathe in the fresh salty air and remember the good, the beautiful, the magical."

But on this morning, the beauty and magic are gone. The colors dulled. I feel no awe. No peace. My chest tightens as my brain calculates the drop. Time to impact. Certainty of the result. It occurs to me that if I die here, my family will not want to scatter my ashes here. That I will ruin this place for them too. I remember a show about a body found on a beach, how so many lives were destroyed by a singular act, and shards of grief and doubt penetrate the darkness inside me. I tell myself if I can just get to the other side of the bluffs and begin climbing up again, I will make it back to my car. And if I make it back to my car, I may survive this day. I don't want to be alive, but I also don't want to die. I just want this, all of this, to stop. My feet are heavy. The air thick. I continue to cry but make it across the bluff and begin to climb.

And then, at the end of the trail, I see my best friend, Deborah, walking toward me. I haven't seen her in over a year, because of Covid. *How odd*, I think, how beyond coincidental she would be here, but then, I see the look on her face and realize it isn't odd or coincidental. She has come to find me.

She opens her arms, hugs me, tells me, "Hold on," and calls someone. "I've got her," she says. She leads me to a bench in the lot at the top of the road and explains that after I left, my husband called our daughter in Minneapolis, and our daughter called her. Deborah has never been to Torrey Pines in her life, but she drove over, asked someone about the trails, made a wild guess as to which one I might be on, and set off. The chances of her finding me, she says, were infinitesimal. I weep as she says, "The universe wants you here. We all want you here."

I ask if my son knows, and Deborah says no, only my daughter. I nod, relieved; then, through the tears, I begin to say I am okay, this was a momentary blip, but she stops me. She says, "No, you're not. You're not okay, Anastasia. I love you, but you're not okay."

And I give up. I hear myself say, "Something is broken inside me and I cannot fix it," and right then I see my husband's truck go by, not far from where I borrowed the phone to text him the *I'm okay* lie. I know that I have hurt him—and my daughter. I cry harder. Say, "I'm so sorry. I'm so sorry."

"Look at me," Deborah says tenderly. "Look at me. You're not okay, but we've got you."

An hour later, I admit the truth to a psych nurse, that for the first time in my life, I wanted to end it. That I had a plan. There is something both earth-shatteringly frightening and freeing about this admission. Within hours, I am talking to a psychologist, signing up for cognitive behavioral therapy classes, speaking to a psychiatrist about medication. With each retelling of the day, I cry anew.

I wish I could say that was it—that I got the help I needed and was miraculously better. But that isn't what happened. Over the next few months, I did engage with the CBT, the talk therapy and meditation, but I resisted taking medication, refusing to believe I needed it. That is, until about six weeks ago, when the storm clouds regathered and the time between thunder and lightning grew alarmingly short. Only then did I begin taking a small oblong blue pill every morning. Only then did the blanket of despair lighten and lift.

And yesterday—yesterday—I went for a hike at Torrey Pines and saw bright blues and greens and purples and whites—the ocean and wildflowers and sandstone cliffs. I breathed in the salty air, felt the breeze on my face, and it was beautiful and magical. Again.

ON ALL SIDES

JANET HAFNER

Author's Note: This story is written by Janet Hafner in the words of her firefighter son.

In the middle of the night, my handheld radio squawked. "Strike Team 9130 Golf, respond to the Cedar Fire."

I gave the standard response to let the commander know I understood: "9130 Golf, Cedar Fire. Copy." It was a blistering October day in 2003 with a gusting fifty-mile-an-hour wind. As I made my way to the barracks, I thought about how this fire was going to test us all.

I was the strike-team leader for two crews of seventeen convicts from the California Department of Corrections who were assigned to an honor camp because of good behavior or time served. For two months, I had trained thirty-four inmates in how to knock down raging blazes and, more importantly, how to survive. Some of these men and women had a couple of seasons under their belts, while others were rookies. All were motivated—every day on the line equaled one day off the time they would be locked up. They knew they had to prove themselves.

I stood at the doorway to their barracks. They slept as if they didn't have anything to worry about.

"Up and at 'em! We've got a job!" I shouted as I flicked the master light switch. Bodies flew off cots into waiting fire gear—fireproof clothing, canteen, fire shelter, helmet, and mask.

"We've got a high-burn index on our hands. Not an easy one to contain. Fire column over one hundred and fifty feet. This is what you've trained for."

25

We prayed

Before loading the buses, two circles formed, heads bowed, as I began the Firefighter's Prayer: "When I am called to duty, God, whenever flames may rage, give me strength to save some life." The prayer ended. In silence, they took their places in the vehicle that would take them to their trial. I hopped in my van, and with the buses snaking behind me, we sped along Highway 15.

Because of global warming, the fire season now lasted eight months instead of five. I glanced in the rearview mirror. Plumes of dense black smoke reminded me of the Pendleton fire. But I could tell that this one, the Cedar Fire, was bigger. *Last report is that it's burning at 2,000 degrees, and the firestorm is sucking up everything in its pat*h.

I could see the fire had exploded into hundreds of acres, forming a blistering red, yellow, and orange wall on both sides of the freeway. It was traveling so fast it easily out-paced the van doing sixty-five. When we arrived at the staging area, five strike teams and all the engines and pumpers listened intently to orders being shouted their way.

"Strike Team 9130 Golf, take your teams to Pine Hills Fire Station."

"Copy that." This'll be a first for the rookies. This'll tell me if their training sunk in.

Fire howled on all sides, fanned by a south wind. *Damn, it's faster by another twenty miles per hour.*

The paved road descended into the valley. I was about a hundred yards ahead of my convict-crew buses. Suddenly, the fire split in two, jumped the road, and formed a solid wall before and after the van. Hundred-foot flames twisted and spun around the thick opaque smoke.

The driver behind me can't see me. He won't know where I am. Gotta keep going. I clamped my trembling fingers around the steering wheel. *Damn, can't see anything past the windshield. Where the hell is the dip? Shit, I'm boxed in.*

I reached for the radio.

"9130 Crew, stay where you are. This is a class-one blaze. I've got to keep going. See if I can get through it. Out."

"Gotcha, boss. We'll catch up with you on the other side," a nervous voice answered.

I hiked my left shoulder up to my ear to shield my face. The heat from the flames penetrated the window glass next to me. My face scorched—felt like it was about to ignite. I couldn't see where I was.

Inch the van forward, veer left—gently, and whatever you do, stay on the road. Don't take your hands off the steering wheel. Keep the engine revved up. Down the hill first—I know how this road is laid out. Now a little to the left. I'm at the dip—the chimney where all the heat and smoke get funneled.

As if I had a partner sitting next to me, I said as loud as I could, "Okay, the road is starting to climb. It'll curve left just about now. The wind wants to push the van—hang on." Devouring flames licked the van top to bottom. My heart slammed against my ribs.

"Damn, my knuckles are burning, but I can't take my hands off the steering wheel. If I drive off the road, I'll be burned alive. Don't stop. Don't stop," I roared over the deafening sound of the snarling, snapping fire.

And then—*wait—is it possible?* Somehow, the galloping wind had blown enough to show me a clearing up ahead—one hundred yards wide and a hundred yards deep. I let out a breath I had been holding onto for dear life as I made my way into the clearing.

I made it. I made it. Now, where're my crews?

In a few minutes, my trained prisoner firefighters arrived. They spilled out of the buses and grabbed their tools—"You have to knock this freakin' fire down. Crew Thirteen, be ready to evac to higher ground. We might have to use our shelters." Behind masks, I couldn't read their faces, but I knew they were terrified.

Chainsaws sprung to life. The crew's job was to cut fire breaks around the structures to save them. The odds of saving homes were very low. Our goal: save the savable.

As the crews fought to hold back the ravenous flames, the fickle wind shifted again.

My radio squawked. *Must be the incident commander.*

"McCain Strike Team, go ahead." My dry mouth could barely spit out the words.

"9130 Golf, get to the apartment complex in Ramona," the incident commander barked.

"Copy. Load 'em up!" I shouted. But we didn't have time to get to the buses. The fire tore up the sides of the canyon surrounding us. It barreled at us.

The incident commander's voice from a bullhorn shouted, "Run for it! Run!"

Another five minutes, and we wouldn't have made it to the apartment. We'd all be dead. *That was close.*

It was well after midnight when a relief team took over. My "swamper" (the top inmate on the crew) collapsed next to a scorched tree—me next to him. Sleep wasn't awaiting us, only rest; the fire could change direction, and we would scramble to our feet, put on our gear, and move. It was three in the morning when a loud crack startled us. A charred branch snapped and came slamming to the earth, inches away from my head. I rolled out of its way. Fireballs fell all around us.

"Damn, Captain, that widow-maker almost had you."

I stood listening to the wind's eerie cry along with the fire's roar and the hand tools scraping the hot earth. When surrounded by fire, you stare in disbelief, but you know it's real. A firestorm is visually spectacular and gut-wrenchingly scary.

One breath filled my body. Not one fatality, and by the time we left, it was ninety-percent contained.

In the space of four days, I almost died three times. My team had done good. I was proud of them.

Two days later, I heard on the radio that one of the firefighters on the Ramona fire had died. A chill ran down my spine. I called my wife and said, "It's not me." I stared at the radio, in thought.

My life had been on the line many times. But somehow, this time was different. At the beginning of the Cedar Fire, it was just another fire. Just another job. But after today . . . it was the first time in all the years in the fire service that I had a heightened awareness of dying. Now, death was more real to me.

A week later, I stood in line in a grocery store in uniform when a man cut in line and got in my face. His eyes were filled with hate; his index finger shot out and struck my chest. He bellowed, "My house burned down in the Cedar Fire! You—you didn't do enough to save my house! It's your fault!"

MODEL STUDENT

ELISE KIM PROSSER, PHD

"Hide your nipple," instructs my Spanish teacher. Mortified, I cross my arms over my chest and feel the tight white blouse constrict. My outgrown rainbow pants are high-waters. I wish I had money to buy new clothes. A pink polo shirt, chinos, and penny loafers might help me fit in with the prepsters at my new high school.

"Sit down on the steps while I get my light meter," he directs. He retrieves a handheld device from his metal photography case. Waving the gadget in front of my face, he sighs.

"Stay here while I get the reflector tripod from the trunk of my car." He marches off to the teachers' parking lot.

Who knew so much of modeling was waiting? I should have gone home, but I'm still here. Last period, I got a B on my Spanish test about *Don Quixote*. I missed a question on imperfect subjunctive diction by Cervantes. I need an A to get into an Ivy League college. After class, I summoned my nerve and approached our teacher, Maestro.

"Is there any way I can earn extra credit?" I asked, looking down at his pointy alligator shoes. "Maybe I could write a paper on Dulcinea, Don's unrequited love. I have to maintain my 4.0 GPA."

Maestro appraised me up and down, then held me in his gaze.

"*Querida,* don't worry your pretty little head," he soothed, patting my shoulder. I glanced into the eyes of the bald, middle-aged Black man wearing a purple velvet three-piece suit.

"*Por supuesto.* I just got a new zoom lens for my camera. I want to try it out before I take yearbook photos," he said. "I need a model. Meet me after school in the woods behind the gym."

29

I nodded with relief. That sounded way more fun than writing a paper. After last bell, I walked to my locker and bumped into my friend Sandy.

"Is it weird Maestro asked me to model after school?" I asked.

"Not really," she answered. "He *is* the school photographer and takes senior portraits. But he also could be a perv."

"I'm sure it's fine. I mean, he teaches at an all-girls school. Plus, I really need an A to get into my dream college," I rationalized.

"You're such a *marron nariz*," she sniffed.

"I am *not* a brown nose. And the adjective goes after the noun in Spanish, duh. That's why you only got a C."

"You're just like Don Quixote, naive and tilting at windmills."

"Then you're my loyal sidekick, Sancho Panza. Come with?" I tried not to appear needy.

"I can't. My mom and I are gonna bake cookies at my house." No one waits for me after school at my apartment. Sandra grinned slyly.

"Hey, how are Maestro and a frog alike?"

"How?"

"They both hop on anything and say *rub it, rub it*." She laughed hysterically. I didn't.

I sauntered through the gym and exited toward the woods. I considered backing out, but Maestro saw me and called me over. He had already set up his photography equipment.

So, I've been waiting on the steps for ten minutes, and now my butt's cold from the concrete. Interrupting my rumination, Maestro returns with the round white reflector tripod. After adjusting the setup, he turns his attention to me.

"*Ahora*, lean on your side." He arranges my arms and legs and tells me to point my hands and feet to create a long line.

"Pretend you're Brooke Shields in the Calvin Klein ad," he directs.

I mimic Brooke in the TV commercial. "You wanna know what comes between me and my Calvins? Nothing." *Kick one leg high into the air.* Brooke is my idol. She's only sixteen like me, but she's a millionaire. In her romantic movie *Endless Love*, she and her boyfriend do it for the first time. Then, her dad makes her break up with him. So, the boyfriend burns down their house and goes to jail. I hope someday a boy will be that wildly in love with me. *Caress my heart.* Martin Hewitt played her boyfriend. He's got a hot bod and will be a superstar. *Peer into the sky.* First-time actor Tom Cruise played the friend. He's forgettable and will never make it big.

"*Guau*, you're a natural," exclaims Maestro, snapping continuously. "You could be a professional. Models earn $100 an hour."

"What? My job pays $3 an hour. Minimum wage." With that much money, I could buy my very own Calvin Klein jeans.

"Have you considered modeling school?" Maestro inquires.

"I've seen ads in *Seventeen* magazine for Barbizon. 'Be a model. Or just look like one,'" I parody. "But I can't afford the tuition."

"You need headshots. I can help you."

My imagination runs wild from his encouragement. The phone rings. Hello? It's Brooke's agent, Eileen Ford. You want to sign me? Move to New York City? *Act excited.* Live in your mansion with Phoebe Cates? *Jump up and down.* Naturally, I'd go by only one name, like supermodels Iman and Gia. *Look over shoulder with haughty expression.*

Clicketa-clicketa-clicketa.

The sound jolts me back to reality. Brooke is six feet tall. I'm only five foot four. Brooke has long flowing locks. I have a frizzy home perm.

"Let's change backgrounds." Maestro leads me to a weeping willow tree.

"Pose under the bent branches. Imagine you're Princess Diana."

"Y'know, I woke up at 4:30 a.m. to watch live news coverage of her royal wedding."

I fantasize that the soft leaves caressing my face form my veil. I'm in the horse-drawn carriage on the way to the cathedral. *Wave at adoring fans.* Next, I'm floating up the aisle in my poufy white wedding dress with a twenty-five-foot-long train. Finally, I reach the altar where Prince Charles awaits. *Kneel and bow head.* Millions around the world watched our fairy-tale wedding, confident we would live happily ever after. *Curtsy with grace.*

Clicketa-clicketa-clicketa.

The noise cuts short my reverie. I don't even have a date for my junior prom. Or money to buy a dress. How will I ever meet a boy at an all-girls school? Who will love me?

"*Preciosa*. You should enter a beauty contest," Maestro advises. "You could win a college scholarship. You need to submit a full-body photo for the bathing suit competition. Last setting." Maestro places me in front of a limestone fountain.

"Act like you're Miss America."

I impersonate a pageant contestant and promenade across the stage. *Shoulders back, hand on hip.* Feign surprise when they announce my win. *Two hands on crown.* Wave to the audience. Mouth "thank you" with fake humility. *Half spin at end of runway.*

"Gorgeous!" he exclaims. No one's ever called me gorgeous before. At least they stopped calling me "four-eyes" ever since I got contacts.

"Now bend over to show your cleavage." Hot flush creeps up my neck. "Squeeze your elbows together." My silver-dollar pancakes squish. Maestro licks his lips.

Clicketa-clicketa-clicketa.

This is a pipe dream. I can't be Miss America. I'm not White. Or blond. Sun-In turned my hair orange.

"The sun is setting. We lost the light. Let's continue at my photography studio."

"Where's that?

"My house. In the basement."

"I dunno." I frown.

"I have a dark room, so I can develop your test shots for free."

"I have to get home." My feet feel like concrete blocks.

"You missed the last bus, but I can drive you." Maestro packs up his equipment. "Help carry this tripod to my car." He walks to the teachers' parking lot. I obediently follow.

We stow the cameras and accessories into his silver Firebird Trans Am. Maestro opens the passenger door for me with chivalry. I get in. He inserts a cassette tape, *Man of La Mancha*, the Broadway musical about Don Quixote. We sing along. "To dream . . . the impossible dream!"

BUT WHO WILL WATCH THE BABY IF I GO TO JAIL?

SAADIA ALI ESMAIL

The stainless-steel blade glistens against the stark white cutting board, my hands clammy as they clench the black handle tightly, my eyes blurring as they try to focus on cutting the tomatoes. The chopped onions are already sizzling on the stove, quickly caramelizing in the saucepan. I'm making my husband's favorite curry, something I haven't done in a long time, not since the baby was born. The skin under my wrist is pale, a vein clearly visible. It would only take one cut, a quick slice. No, what am I thinking? I need to cook; I have a newborn, a husband. I'm a daughter, a sister, a friend.

I remember what my friend Cyndy had said when she visited a few days ago. I had just confided my terrifying thoughts out loud and needed her reassurance that I wasn't losing it. She knew me and would tell me I could never do such a thing.

"Do you know why I never wear short-sleeve shirts?" she asked me, as I sat next to her on the sofa, weeping uncontrollably. I shook my head, blubbering a no.

"Because I once tried to stab myself."

I stopped wiping my nose and looked at her in disbelief. "You? You tried to kill yourself?" She just nodded and held my hand. It was odd but comforting to know that I was not alone in my thoughts and that others were just as emotionally disturbed as me. *Would we always be like this, though?* Would we end up like the experiments that so often failed in the labs of the science startup we both worked for?

33

Now, with my husband finally back at work, I'm in the kitchen, alone, and my newborn baby girl is asleep in the bedroom. My husband finally went back to work this morning.

"Are you sure you'll be okay? I can stay and work from home . . ." Ali was trying so hard to understand, but now I could see even he was concerned. I told him each and every thought. But I need to let it out. When I say the words aloud and tell him the clips from my horror movie, it all sounds so delusional.

"No, just get back to work; you can't stay home forever. I'll be fine," I had insisted. *But I wasn't.* If Cyndy could try slicing herself, so could I. She was far stronger than me, and yet, she had tried it. But she had failed. I quickly put the knife down, turn off the stove with the onions now burnt, and hurry to the sofa in the living room, burying my face in the cushions, sobbing once more.

***

The postpartum depression had started when our baby was barely six weeks old. We were returning home after taking my in-laws sightseeing. As our apartment's parking garage gate had opened, I glanced over at my baby and thought just how perfect she was: her face, her cheeks, her little hands. *What would it feel like if I cut off one of her fingers?* As soon as we parked, I quickly stepped out of the car, averting my gaze from her car seat and letting my mother-in-law take care of her for the rest of the day, giving the excuse that my head was aching.

"Ali, I had this crazy thought yesterday." I woke up early the next morning and described it to him. *How could I not tell him?* He just laughed, gave me a hug, and said I could never do such a thing. I couldn't even harm a fly.

Then why did that disturbing thought come to my mind?

A few days after that first image, I sat on the living room recliner with my daughter in my lap. Staring at her long fingers, I told my mother-in-law about the horrific scenes swirling in my head. I was doing something far worse than just cutting off my baby's fingers. The

34

images played out in my mind as if I were a psychopathic butcher in a thriller movie.

"Try, just try pulling one of her fingers right now," my mother-in-law had said. I had just stared at her, then the baby, and caressed her hand, her face.

"See, you can't even pull a finger. Do you think you could do anything worse?" She was right; I always had a calm temperament and never hurt anyone. But then, why did these thoughts keep coming?

My mother-in-law got up from her spot on the sofa, patted my hand, and matter-of-factly said, "Go get some help. You need to enjoy these days with your baby. They will be gone before you know it. Even if you have to take some medicine, do it. Don't miss this time." She was so nonjudgmental, something I had known, yet was still in awe of, ever since I married her son. It was a different story when I confided in my mother.

"You're crazy. Just say some prayers, and you'll be fine." *If prayers alone could do something, then why would I have continued pleading with God for some respite, some assurance that this was just a test?*

And my father's advice?

"Go see a doctor, take whatever medicine they prescribe. My doctor has been telling me for years to take antidepressants, but I never did." *If only you had, how different would life have been?* How could I heed his advice when he still went sullen and silent for days without reason?

I went to see a psychiatrist and started an antidepressant, Zoloft. I couldn't believe it: me, an educated woman with a close network of friends and family; me, a successful first-generation American Muslim woman who believed in the power of prayer; me, now on a drug that would alter my mind so that I could be happy again, so that my mind would function without psychotic thoughts. *This can't be me.* After all, my name, Saadia, means happy, lucky. Maybe I shouldn't have laughed when the nurse had explained the postpartum blues to me right before I was discharged from the hospital.

"No, I don't think I'll ever get depressed. My husband makes me laugh all day."

***

Two weeks later, and the Zoloft still has not kicked in. The thoughts of hurting my child are interspersed with suicidal thoughts, and I'm not sure which is worse. I'm jumping off the balcony. I'm drowning my baby in the tub. I'm cutting my wrist with a knife.

"Ali, they're taking me away." I had woken up in a cold sweat.

"What, who's taking you, where?" Ali's voice was groggy with sleep.

"The police, they're putting handcuffs on me. Tell them to stop; I didn't do anything."

"You're just dreaming," and he held me tight as the images floated in and out.

"But who will watch the baby if I go to jail?" The words sounded ludicrous as they spilled out of my mouth, my mind saying, *there is no baby; you've already killed her.* I shuddered, clutched Ali's hand, and fell into a fitful sleep.

I need to stop. I need to finish cooking while the baby is still asleep. I cast the sofa cushion aside, and my eyes wander to a picture of myself in a collage framed on the wall, one in which my hair is blowing wildly, my smile big, my teeth flashing.

I go back into the kitchen, take a deep breath, dump the knife in the kitchen sink, and finish cooking the curry. Though I have no appetite, at least I'll lose the pregnancy weight faster; something good can come out of this. *If I survive.*

I feel as if I'm a small sapling stuck in a raging river after an unexpected thunderstorm. I look to onlookers like I can easily swim in the currents, but only I know what I am enduring. Only I can hope to be washed ashore to plant my roots, to grow the branches of my family.

After a while, something settles in me, and I find a way to go with the flow, to see that I'm not as alone as I often think. I find some peace knowing that others out there have survived what I faced and have the scars to prove it.

***

Fifteen years and seven episodes of depression later, I'm still here. It hasn't been easy: the thoughts, the images, the feeling that I'm going to become a cold-blooded killer and end up in an isolated psychiatric ward. Knives were picked up countless times, and wrists bared as if on a cold dissection table. I know it's just a mind game. And I've won every time. So far.

MR. GREENSLEEVES

CHILI CILCH

I stared at the grasshopper, amazed that he had perched just a few inches from my face. His sleek body glowed emerald green in the TV light. He had been sitting on the wall across from me above the TV. I hadn't noticed him hop across to land on the plant next to me. I picked up the remote and paused Jane Fonda in mid-sentence. *Who is this grasshopper watching Netflix with me? Who are you really, Mr. Greensleeves?*

Mr. Greensleeves seemed to quiver in reply. I leaned in closer to him and whispered, "Dad, is it you?"

Dad had been gone just over a year, but I had really lost him two years before. A paralyzing stroke changed him in ways both beautiful and wretched. Gone was the father I adored. For almost two years, we cared for a profoundly sweet eighty-nine-year-old child. I helped to change his adult diapers and reposition him to prevent bedsores. I wondered if it embarrassed him. He would repeatedly thank me, and I'd tell him, "You don't have to thank me, Daddy, 'cause you're the best dad in the world."

"I am?" he'd reply, his big brown eyes filled with the wonder of an innocent, causing my own eyes to brim with tears.

My whole life, I'd been accused of being just like my father. The accuser's intent was not to flatter, but I'd smile and think, *thank God.* We shared a love of politics, quantum physics, and art.

He'd frequently call me to solicit my assistance.

"Hi, honey, I'm working on a book on San Diego's unsung heroes, wondering if you can help me out with a bit of research."

"Dad, I hardly have time for my own projects. What did you have in mind?"

Squinting at my TV-watching grasshopper, I recalled the muggy September day I found him. I'd come home from work and immediately stripped down to my bra and panties. *When did San Diego get so damn humid?* I moved the shower curtain aside to turn on the cold water. Against the white subway tiles, he appeared vividly green, a bright Kermit-the-Frog hue of happiness. *What the heck—where did you come from?* The name popped into my head and flew out of my mouth. "Hello, Mr. Greensleeves."

Surprisingly, he didn't move.

"I'm not going to hurt you, but you might want to step away from the shower."

Getting out of the shower, I reached for a towel and scanned the walls, looking for my green friend. He must have bounced off. *Smart grasshopper, he took my advice.*

I slipped on my robe and surveyed my home, finally finding him on the wall above the sliding glass door to my balcony. I opened the door so he could escape. He landed just outside of the screen door.

"Thanks for visiting, Mr. Greensleeves."

I thought for sure he had returned to the wild, until I saw him on the dining room wall.

"Did you decide to stay the night?"

Perhaps a scary predator lurked outside. A bird? I had seen some raucous, wild parrots in the trees across from my balcony. *Are grasshoppers even aware of dangerous predators?*

The next day, I added a new task to my morning ritual: the search for my little green man. I'd call out his name and we'd play a delightful game of hide-and-go-seek.

After a week, I realized my home lacked sources of nourishment for an insect. I googled grasshoppers and discovered that people did keep them as pets, typically in glass aquariums. I decided against an aquarium. What if I damaged his tiny legs trying to catch him? I didn't want to permanently injure the poor bugger. I also learned grasshoppers could live up to three years in captivity. "Hey, Mr. Greensleeves, when's your birthday?" How does one discern the age of an insect? It's not like a vet could check his teeth. I closed my laptop. I needed to find some grasshopper chow.

Walking through the nursery's rows of plants, I nodded to a young man wearing a Walter Anderson's shirt. He smiled and asked, "Can I help you?"

"Yes, I'm interested in knowing what kind of food to feed a grass-hopper."

"Right, we do have plants that repel insects. Follow me, this way."

"Oh no, I want something for my grasshopper to eat."

He gave me a quizzical look. "That's a first. Most folks want to know how to get rid of them." He led me to rows of various salad greens and I selected a pack of Butterhead lettuce.

The next day, I examined the lettuce leaves to see if I could detect any nibbles. At first, I didn't see anything. A leaf tickled my nose as I leaned closer. What I saw made me laugh. "You're eating, Mr. Greens-leeves." The leaves were perforated with tiny delicate bites that looked like half-moon smiles.

My grasshopper seemed happy living free-range in my house. His Facebook pictures garnered tons of likes, and friends suggested I teach him tricks. I'd gleefully imagined a miniature circus of trained grasshoppers.

During the last week of October, about eight weeks since Mr. Greensleeves started rooming with me, I began assembling my Day of the Dead altar. I'd been honoring my deceased loved ones by creating shrines ever since I participated in a Dia de los Muertos art show in 1987. The jewel of my installation was a sixteen by twenty-four-inch canvas covered in Chicklets squares of candied chewing gum that I had painstakingly glued like miniature mosaic tiles to form the image of the Virgin of Guadalupe. I'd always been fascinated by religion, even though my father raised me to be a science-minded atheist. I loved Mexico's Day of the Dead tradition, annually honoring the dearly departed with storytelling, music, and their favorite foods and libations. As I got older, the pictures on my altar expanded with pictures of family and friends who had passed on too soon. But this year, I'd be adding my daddy as the altar's centerpiece.

I'd talk to each person as I dusted off their framed photographs and placed them on the altar. I saved Dad for last.

"You look so handsome in your uniform, Daddy," I said, placing his picture on the swath of purple velvet to symbolize his Purple Heart medal from WWII.

"Remember the time I broke my arm at the veterans parade, and a police car drove you back to the store?" I laughed at the memory, waving to my dad as he rode in the back like he'd been apprehended, as I waited for a friend to take me to the ER.

The doorbell rang and I called out from the kitchen, "Come on in, it should be open."

I'd invited my family over to see the altar. My brother Ken came in with my mother on his arm, followed by my sister Jennifer. As they gazed at the photographs, I poured them each a shot.

"What's this?" my mother asked, wrinkling her nose.

"Tequila, but I should be serving Dad's and my favorite drink, Manhattans."

I pointed up to the wall above the altar. "You haven't met Mr. Greensleeves. I'm beginning to tame him."

My sister Jennifer looked at me incredulously, one eyebrow raised.

"Watch, I'll show you," I said, taking a Tiger Lily stem from the vase of flowers. I held it up to Mr. Greensleeves. He slowly made his way on his spindly legs onto the flower, and I lowered the stem back into the vase. "See?!" I exclaimed triumphantly.

On the night Mr. Greensleeves hopped over to watch TV with me, it reminded me of all the times I'd stay up late with Dad, watching *Saturday Night Live* and Uri Geller bending spoons with his mind on Tom Snyder's late show.

I'm not a religious person, but I am a spiritual one. Mr. Greensleeves isn't the first insect I've looked at and thought, *Do I know you?* I'm not sure where I got the notion; maybe in a college religious studies class, or maybe some book gave me the idea. If the dead wanted a short-term stay in this temporal world, wouldn't possessing a fly, ladybug, or grasshopper be a convenient mode to check in on loved ones and get an earthly life energy fix? As I peered at Mr. Greensleeves, he inched a bit closer to me. I suddenly felt a warm energy cascading through my body from the crown of my head.

"Good to watch TV with you again, Dad."

41

In early December, I couldn't find Mr. Greensleeves. Calling out his name, I searched all the walls and curtains and looked to see if he was on one of his lettuce leaves. Then I saw him on the floor. Tears clouded my vision as I gingerly picked him up.

I found a jewelry box to serve as his casket. One day, I will paint and bedazzle his faded green body, restoring his resplendent beauty. He'll look handsome, prominently displayed on my Dias de los Muertos altar. My rainbow connection to a very special grasshopper. I will gaze at the framed faces of the ones I miss so terribly but choose to believe, *you're still here, aren't you?*

CIRCLED

KIMBERLY JOY

The wind sprayed salt water in my face as Taga, a short, stocky Chamorro, expertly drove the dive boat away from the safety of the shore. Our destination: a place where the ocean floor dropped off, creating a sheer wall that descended thousands of feet into the deep, deep blue sea. I felt sick, not from the rough bouncing of the boat over choppy waters, but because of the quivering apprehension in my belly. I'd scuba-dived many times before in Guam, but this would be the first time without the security of an experienced divemaster. It would be just me and my dive partner, Michelle, a woman known for her previous diving mishaps.

The boat slowed, the engine shut off, and silence filled the air. We had arrived. Taga threw the heavy anchor over the side. No turning back now.

Another boat was anchored a few yards away. Three divers appeared at its back deck, hauling up spearfishing equipment. It didn't look like they'd caught anything. *Good,* I thought, *no blood in the water to attract sharks.*

As we prepared our equipment, I scrutinized Michelle, wishing I had a more competent dive partner. I knew that of the two of us, I would have to lead.

I expected we would see colorful triggerfish, clowns, parrots, and gobies, just like I'd seen on other dives, nothing out of the ordinary. But I dictated our dive plan to Michelle twice to make sure she understood. We moved to the edge of the boat, put on our fins and buoyancy vests, and adjusted our masks. I put my regulator in and heard the familiar sounds of my oxygen tank-dependent Darth Vadar-sounding breath. Michelle and I took a final look at each other, placed a hand over our masks and regulators to keep them secure, then fell backward off the boat, splashing into the water.

Going first, I slowly released the air from my vest and descended along the anchor line. I saw Michelle dropping from above, reflected sunlight creating a brilliant halo around her. Reaching eighty feet, we swam toward the wall, skimming along the ocean floor. Until, up ahead, it looked as if that floor disappeared.

I slowed the pace—and then we were upon it. The ocean floor ended abruptly at a sharp ninety-degree angle. I hovered at the edge and looked down. I'd never seen such vast, endless space, dark and ominous. My stomach dropped.

I looked at Michelle. We checked our depth gauges, and I signaled one, two, zero with my fingers, reminding her we would dive to 120 feet, then ascend back to eighty feet for the rest of the dive. My heart raced as I swam over the edge and, tipping head down, began to descend. Enormous, magnificent sea fans clung to the wall, swaying with the current opening before us, in brilliant coral orange, lavender, and sea green. I was mesmerized. Checking my depth gauge, I saw we were at 120 feet, our maximum depth.

Turning right and expecting to see Michelle, my chest constricted as I saw her dropping down into the darkness. Michelle was petite, susceptible to being "narced," a condition in which nitrogen builds up in the blood, causing confusion and impaired judgment. *Shit.* I kicked hard to catch up to her, watching my depth gauge as I descended—125 feet—130—135. Finally, I reached the tip of her fin and yanked it to get her attention. *Up!* I jabbed my finger upward. She looked dazed but followed me toward the top of the wall.

Back at eighty feet, cresting the top of the ridge, I glanced backward quickly to make sure Michelle was still with me. As my eyes returned forward, a giant green moray eel slithered out of a coral crevice inches from my face. A large school of triggerfish abruptly scattered in all directions. An eerie sensation washed over me. *Huh, weird. What the? Fuck!*

Straight in front of me was a massive hammerhead shark. At least ten feet long. Thick. Muscular. Barrel-like. Its body was perpendicular to mine, and I was on a collision course, swimming right for it. A small, beady black eye rolled around in the middle of the gray, fleshy cone that protruded from its head, looking directly at me. I took in the rows of vicious teeth, jutting buck-toothed from its mouth. I'd seen plenty of reef sharks before, but those looked slender, even graceful, compared to the monster in front of me.

I stopped—floating—suspended. *Holy shit, holy shit, what do I do?* My thoughts came like machine gunfire. *He's going to eat us. What do I do? What do I do?*

An inner voice of calm bubbled up inside me. *First, you need to breathe—just breathe. You're using a regulator; you can't hold your breath.* Until that moment, I hadn't realized I'd been holding my breath. *What do you do if a shark attacks? Punch them in the nose. Yes. Punch them in the nose.* I looked again at the menacing rows of teeth directly under his nose. *That's ridiculous?! I'm not putting my hand near those teeth.* I thought of the small dive knife strapped to my calf—*Like that's going to work. That'll just piss him off.*

In that instant, I realized there was nothing I could do.

I couldn't problem-solve my way out. Any fantasy of control disintegrated with that truth. I knew that if the shark wanted to attack, it would. Acceptance washed over me. The underwater world became bright and vivid, the ocean a translucent aqua blue, the shark's skin a dark gray-brown. It was as if time had stopped, and I existed only in the present moment. I was free from fear. My muscles relaxed, and my breath slowed—a sense of complete calm, almost a state of serenity, flowed through me, leaving me with a pure presence of being and only one thought—*all I can do is watch it. Just watch it.*

As I came back into my body, I realized I'd been doing just that. I'd kept my eyes locked on the shark, turning slowly to my right to keep it in sight. *It's circling us.* I watched and turned until I'd rotated 180 degrees and now faced Michelle, who'd been behind me. She had not caught sight of the shark that was now directly behind her. I locked eyes with her. I pointed behind her, dramatically using my right hand to imitate a fin on top of my head. She looked at me and—waved. *What?*

Come on! I tried again, desperately needing her to understand. Frantic, I continued pointing, making the shark signal over and over. Finally, she looked behind her. Her body jerked in a spasm of fear as she saw the shark only a few feet from her. Reacting to her sudden movement, the shark thrashed about; its head lurched to the right while its hind body violently twisted left. The metallic taste in my mouth returned. *Oh my God, it's going to eat her!*

Time stopped again. And then—miraculously—the hammerhead began to move slowly AWAY from us. Overwhelming relief flooded through me. *It's swimming away. It's swimming away.* But the relief was short-lived. I remembered that hammerheads usually swam in schools, and we were at the edge of a wall that dropped miles into the depths of the ocean, home to giant creatures of the deep. I had no intention of waiting around for its buddies to show up. We needed to get out of there.

Michelle and I converged, our eyes big as saucers. UP, I pointed, UP! Michelle nodded. I pointed to our dive watches and depth gauges. We wanted to get to the surface quickly, but we'd been so deep we needed to control our ascent and make a decompression stop—at fifteen feet for three minutes—or risk getting decompression sickness, also deadly. The adrenaline pumping through my system powered me toward the dark silhouette of the underside of our boat, just visible in the distance. Arriving at the anchor line, we ascended slowly until we reached fifteen feet, where we waited—floating—bobbing. I jumped at every shadow. I imagined an entire school of hammerheads appearing at any moment. I wondered which would be worse, dying from decompression sickness or being eaten by a hammerhead. Terrified, I waited. The seconds moved like minutes—tick, tick, tick.

Finally, my dive watch registered three minutes. I ascended the last few feet up toward the sun shining through the water, burst through the surface, grabbed the deck at the rear of the boat, pulled myself up quickly, spit out my regulator, ripped off my mask and fins, and threw them—then myself—into the boat. Michelle was right behind me.

Taga lounged on the driver's seat, eyes closed, face turned up to the sun. He leisurely opened his eyes. "Why you back so soon?"

"Shark, big shark," I sputtered breathlessly.

"You afraid?" he chided. "I see sharks all the time. How big, this shark? What kind?"

"Big. A hammerhead. At least ten feet."

Taga's expression changed to legitimate shock and concern. "Oh, big! Good, you get out early."

Taga pulled in the anchor, and we headed toward shore. My mind replayed the scene over and over: the shark, the eye, the teeth, the fear. I forced myself to breathe. The rhythmic bouncing of the boat and the warm, salty air eventually allowed me to relax, and my fear turned into gratitude—at least it had only been one shark and not an entire school.

Only later would I learn—

hammerheads travel in schools—

but they hunt alone.

THE COURTYARD

LISA CHURCHVILLE

I snuck into Moore's Cancer Center today. I'm sitting in the beautiful open-air courtyard. They still have teak chairs speckled throughout this green oasis in the center of the building. It's not busy today, so I only feel a little guilty for taking up one of the few cushioned seats in the shade by a tall cluster of bamboo. We talked about everything out here. Except I never told you about that first day.

"Call me when you can," was all you wrote in your text. I took a deep breath and dialed back. I looked around my kitchen, noting the champagne bottles that should go to the recycling bin, the drooping basil plant that needed water, and the stack of mail left to open.

I knew you were about to deliver bad news, and still, my body clenched when you told me the doctor wanted you to start chemo right away. We had hoped the hormone treatments would work a little longer. We stuck to the basics of date, time, and where you needed to go. I shook my head and sighed as I put the phone down. I stared out the kitchen window to the yard.

I thought back to meeting you when I was eighteen and how you immediately adopted me as the little sister you always wanted, introducing me to wine and an array of stinky cheese, vegetables in pasta, blues music, off-beat movies, and LA bars. How we shared Polish Christmas, lobster dinners in Rosarito, the birth of your children, and all things girl. How we confided in one another about work and relationship dramas—the stuff you don't share with your husband, kids, or parents. And yet, I couldn't believe I had just offered to take you to that first appointment.

I'm not a caretaker. By choice, I don't have children or pets. I almost pass out when I give blood or think about giving blood. I'm the one friends come to when they want to vent about their husbands, teens, or mothers-in-law. I'm the girl who goes out for a martini to brainstorm how to ask for a raise. I'll even go to the sex store in the seedy part of town to find goodies for a bachelorette party. But caretaking—that's not me. I've easily said no to helping a friend change bandages after a nose job, watching a toddler that isn't potty trained, and babysitting an infant so the parents could have dinner with a prominent politician. But I could never say no to you.

On the day of your appointment, I pulled the car over to the curb and parked two blocks from your house in Ocean Beach. I turned down the radio because the upbeat music grated my nerves. *What had I gotten myself into? Could I keep it together when I saw you?*

I longed to call someone, anyone. I scrolled through the contact list on my phone, and I dismissed them all one by one. The right side of my shirt was wet with sweat. I searched around for anything I could use to dry off a little. I found a napkin smashed into the cup holder beside my seat. I smoothed it out, slipped it under my shirt against my armpit, and cried.

Tears streamed down my face, but the feeling part of me—the part that experiences and can name the emotion—that part was somewhere else. It's a strange thing to be both in your body and out of it at the same time. Like that part was in the car watching me from above but purposely keeping itself at a distance. It was probably better that way. I was here to support you. I didn't allow myself to think about what you felt that day. I wiped my tears, fixed my mascara in the mirror, and continued to your house.

We sat in the waiting room, sipping our drinks from Peet's. It was a good thing we stopped on the way because when you checked in, we found out you needed blood drawn and tested to see if you qualified for chemo that day. The blond woman in scrubs explained if the hemoglobin levels aren't high enough in a twenty-four-hour period before the chemo is to be administered, it's a no-go. Waiting for the results added an extra hour to our stay.

I hoped you couldn't hear my heart racing when the woman called your name. I mentally pulled up my big-girl pants, smiled at the nurse, and followed you to the infusion center. I expected a bunch of frail bald folks sitting in a circle of chairs hooked up to IVs, as I had seen in the movie *50/50*. But it wasn't like that. The room felt the size of a football field. Bright and sunny. Not the drab beige I was expecting. Each patient had personal space—a comfy reclining chair and TV, warm blankets, pillows, and long purple curtains on three sides for privacy.

You didn't tell me you had come in a few days before to get a port in your upper chest. I began to squirm in my chair when the nurse started to take the bandage off. I'd never seen a port before, and it looked painful in that spot by your clavicle. I didn't want to watch you get the shot of pain medication or the blood drawn. I bit my lip and looked away. I felt faint. Now was not the time to be the needy one.

Once that was done, we had that hour to kill. We found a café on the top floor and also this courtyard. We brought snacks here and lounged on these deep wood chairs. We donned sunglasses and stripped down to tank tops to enjoy the rays. It was almost like hanging out with our magazines and cold drinks at the pool.

We returned to the infusion center once the test results came in. You reclined in a chair with the blood pressure cuff around your leg. The nurse explained everything the first-timer needed to know—premeds, possible side effects, scheduling appointments, getting blood drawn the night before so you wouldn't have to wait, and foods to avoid. I remember our surprise that Twinkies made the approved list, but seemingly healthy things like sushi and fresh lettuce did not. She answered every question we asked and made it seem like you were her only patient that day.

There was so much time to pass waiting for the meds to drip from the IV bag. You showed me your new favorite nail polish: My Private Jet by OPI. We talked about your rescue dog, my aging mom, and the huge boobs on my brother's new girlfriend. We giggled when we realized the older male patient on the other side of the curtain was getting an earful. And I realized I just had to be myself. Sitting at chemo could be like sitting at a bar—the same girls, the same topics, just spending time—minus the booze, of course.

I miss our standing date here on Friday mornings—me rolling in with Starbucks, you checking work email, then gabbing about my job search, your boys' last soccer game, and where we were headed to lunch. Even when the days got harder, and you had to hold my arm to go inside, when I had to tell the doctor you were forgetting things, and when on that last day you could only express your love for me by looking into my eyes, I knew I was the lucky one. I had the gift of nothing left unsaid.

Once in a while, I come here to the courtyard to bask in the sun of your memory.

ON OUR WAY

LAURA L. ENGEL

"Good luck finding some guy who wants a woman like you with these kids hanging all over you."

Here we were, exploding into yet another violent shouting match in 1977. Items thrown, threats made. *Find some guy? That was the last thing I needed.* A voice deep inside of me screamed, "No more!"

Our marriage had become a tenuous house of cards. My disgust for the crumbs I had settled for finally surpassed my fear of being alone. What kind of example was this for our three sons?

My husband moved in with his parents—plans that did not include us, which left me with the boys, our home, and a mortgage. After being a stay-at-home mom for ten years, I had no means of my own. We lived thousands of miles away from my family. Friends worried when word got out that we were heading toward divorce.

"What are you going to do? You'll never make it on your own," they were quick to remind me.

"You'll have to move back here," was the mantra from my Mississippi family. I had always put on a brave face so no one knew the real story of our marriage—the real struggle it had been. In a hard-headed fog of denial, I ignored the fact that I was close to destitute.

As my bank account dwindled, reality smacked me in the face. Our house was slipping into foreclosure, and my soon-to-be ex didn't answer my calls. I needed money to feed my children.

I anxiously checked through newspaper want ads each day, which only caused more worry. *I have no work experience. I don't even have the right kind of clothes. What will I do with my sons while I am working?*

I was careful to buy only essentials: milk, eggs, and bread. Filling my VW Bug with gas at sixty-eight cents a gallon became a feat. Late at night, when I sat awake for hours, the boys tucked in bed, I fretted. *Other women found jobs and raised children without men. I could do this. Couldn't I?*

A friend casually mentioned public assistance. I was adamant. "I am not a welfare case."

But I soon realized my kids mattered more than my pride.

***

"You need to sign here." The disgruntled social services clerk pushed papers toward me. I glanced at my little boys' faces, taking in their wide, anxious eyes as all three huddled together on the metal chair beside me. Two-year-old Ian was fussy. His arms reached for me as he sat on nine-year-old Dustin's lap. I squeezed his little hand to comfort him. My middle son Marc watched me with anxious eyes. *Food stamps. How did I get here?* I tried to assure him with a smile and turned back, signing the papers, feeling like the most worthless mother in the world.

"Thank you." I smiled at the clerk. No smile back.

He pushed the food coupon booklet toward me. "You'll get more in the mail. Oh, and don't forget," he sneered, "you can only buy food with these. You can't use them for alcohol or cigarettes."

I herded my sons into the parking lot. The boys plied me with questions. "Why did it take so long, Mom? Who was that grumpy old man? Why did we go there anyway?"

Driving straight to the grocery store to trade the vouchers for much-needed groceries, I splurged on two half-gallons of ice cream. The boys jostled each other, asking for gum or candy at the checkout stand. "Not this time, boys. Look, we have cookies-and-cream and chocolate mint. Your favorites!"

Secretly, I worried, *would the vouchers cover ice cream?* I only had three dollars and change in my wallet.

***

I dressed with care for my first-ever interview, borrowing my girlfriend's stylish sweater dress and matronly pumps, my hair held back with a headband. I was ushered into a stark office and sat in a cold leather chair across from a stern HR executive. I was petrified but put a smile on my face, my heart hammering, and demurely crossed my legs at my ankles while I studied the nameplate on his desk. *John Lee.* His frown lines deepened as he scrutinized my job application.

"Hmph, you're from Mississippi? How did you end up here in Southern California?"

"Um, yes, sir. I was born and raised there, but I married a man from San Diego." I held my shaking hands tight in my lap. "I recently separated from my husband and need a job."

Did he smirk?

"You have no experience. No education." He shook his head. "No work history at all. What have you been doing for the last ten years?"

Caught off guard, I blurted out, "Raising my three boys."

After a few condescending remarks, he abruptly ended the interview. "We don't have the time it would take to train you. You are definitely not what *our* company is looking for."

"Thank you for your time, sir." I stood, deflated, extending my hand. Mr. Lee ignored it.

I hurried down the hallway, my cheeks burning, holding back tears. A young man with fiery red hair, his suit and tie immaculate, was taken by surprise as I slammed into him.

"Sorry, sorry." I glanced up into his blue eyes. "Jerry?"

"Laura? Wow, what are *you* doing here?"

We both laughed. We hadn't seen each other since high school in Mississippi, eleven years before. Jerry immediately steered me into an empty office, where we began to catch up on each other's lives. I tried to sound upbeat, but how could I, with my life such a mess?

"I'm desperate, Jerry. I need a job. Mr. Lee doesn't think I'm trainable."

I was clueless to the drumroll of synchronicity that began its faint rat-a-tat-tat.

How could I have known Jerry was an executive for this company and was in town overseeing the San Diego office for only two days?

Jerry walked me straight back into that gloomy office with his arm around my shoulders. Mr. Lee sprang to his feet.

"Hey, John. This is my old friend Laura. She needs a job, and I want her hired today. Oh, and by the way, John, she is very trainable." Jerry winked at me.

"Yes, sir. Uh, of course," Mr. Lee stuttered, the charade of a smile plastered on his face.

That was how I landed my first job at a large insurance company within a month after the welfare office. The first thing I did was foolishly call and cancel future food stamps.

"Are you sure you want to discontinue them?" The clerk sounded dubious.

I was so smug, proudly stating, "I have a job. I won't be needing them."

It only took a couple of paychecks to realize I was in the same sinking ship I had been in before getting a job. Earning minimum wage, $2.65 an hour, barely covered living expenses. Daycare and after-school care took half of my take-home pay. Close to losing the roof over our heads, I beat myself up for discontinuing the food stamps every time I bought groceries.

As a junior file clerk, I worked long hours pulling dusty manila folders from floor-to-ceiling shelves and rushing them to thirty demanding, mostly male, claims adjusters. At twenty-eight, I was the "old lady" in that entry-level job, working alongside eighteen- and nineteen-year-old girls. I drove home each night through freeway traffic, gathered my boys, started dinner, and helped with schoolwork, ending with baths and bedtime, while my coworkers lingered at happy hour.

As my boys and I settled down one evening, my oldest son, Dustin, leaned against me on the couch and quietly asked, "Mom, when do we get back to normal again?"

"Isn't this normal?" Marc asked from the floor, where he cuddled our cat, Chester. "Normal!" Ian jubilantly called out, pushing his toy fire truck across the rug.

I gave my boys my brightest smile.

"Don't worry, boys, we'll make it."

Deep down inside, I knew we would.

THE TAKEOVER

MARVELYN BUCKY

On a cool autumn morning, I had been working the teller line at a station where the key kept sticking in the cash drawer. I had to squeeze so hard to make the key catch in the lock, I was starting to get a blister on the soft inner tips of my fingers.

The moment it happened, I was going back and forth with this obnoxious man who was withdrawing $300 but refused to give me his ID. I had my hand on my hip, trying to appear taller and more confident than I actually was, and repeated again, "Sir, unfortunately, we need ID to withdraw funds, and I'm sure you can appreciate—"

Suddenly, four masked gunmen stormed through the double doors. Firecracker bursts erupted *pop-pop-pop* as they fired into the ceiling and shouted, "Everybody get down! Everybody get down!"

They looked like mercenary fighters on a battlefield, shrouded in black. My heart thudded in my chest. The obnoxious customer hit the floor. My coworker barricaded herself behind her metal trash can.

But I didn't get down.

I just stood there, stupidly clutching that withdrawal slip in my fist, my brain stuck in a loop of getting my client's ID.

The short their leapt the teller counter like a track star gone rogue. With military precision, he stalked his way down the teller line, grabbing cash and slamming drawers.

As the sounds echoed closer and closer, a voice in my head ricocheted *get down, get down, get down.*

I don't remember moving but quickly found myself on the floor, breathing in the dusty 1980s hunter-green carpet.

My thoughts swirled. This was definitely not on my to-do list for the day.

I pictured my husband's face, my high school sweetheart I had married the previous summer, knowing I might never see him again.

I thought of grabbing my purse with the measly thirty dollars I had left and sprinting to hide out in the bathroom. But this was logistically impossible.

If I tried to run, I'd be shot.

I knew I should reach up and press the silent alarm, but I was too afraid.

Hoping some unknown hero would rise up and foil the bad guys, I curled into myself, squeezing my eyes shut tight, trying to be invisible.

This obviously didn't work, because within minutes the stocky gunman was standing over me. The vice grip of his hard boots pressed into my rib cage on either side. *Please, God, please don't let him step on me.*

I was all of one hundred five pounds and only five foot three. He could easily have crushed me with one blow.

"Where's the key?" he demanded, in a deep baritone. Saying absolutely nothing and keeping my head down, I slowly raised my arm and handed him my teller key.

I envisioned the key sticking in the lock and the robber angrily grabbing my hair and shooting me in the head with his cold metal gun.

I held my breath, bracing for the click of the trigger pull.

Miraculously, the drawer opened, and cash floated to the floor. I could hear labored breathing as the robber tried to grasp falling bills in his hands.

I actually felt sorry for him because he seemed kind of clumsy and wasn't doing a great job of getting the money in his bag.

Within seconds, one of his buddies said, "Hey, times up—we gotta go!"

Before he left, the robber ironically said, "Thanks," as if I had provided some kind of helpful service.

I'm not much of a crier, but when the FBI agent asked, "Where are the victim tellers?" I burst into tears. *Who did he think he was, calling me a victim?*

In the bank lobby during the FBI interview, I had to relive every detail, including reenacting the position I was lying in on the floor. The agent kept saying things like, "What do you mean, he was clumsy?" As if he didn't believe anything I was saying. Like *I* had robbed the bank. I went from tears to hot anger. I wanted to tell him off, but of course, I didn't.

As the FBI team explained the stages we would go through over the next few days, from fear, to anger, to paranoia, I reasoned that this would not affect me.

But on the way home when I stopped off to buy groceries, everyone in the store seemed like a pickpocket out to get me. When a middle-aged woman casually bumped into me, I shouted, "Hey, watch it!" She looked at me in alarm and hurried away.

As shoppers swarmed around me, I developed a terrible pressure in my head and had this overwhelming desire to flee. I stood in the aisle, trying to decide which pasta was the best deal, telling myself *you are being ridiculous.*

But all of the people, loud elevator music, and bright fluorescent lights were too much, so I left without buying anything.

We ended up having canned soup for dinner instead of the spaghetti and salad I had planned. My husband tried to console me, saying, "I like minestrone," but all I tasted was bitter metal residue in my mouth.

That night, as I was trying to write my twenty-page Shakespeare paper, which was due within days, the phone kept ringing.

My alarmed mother said, "You have to quit!" But I had bills to pay, so this was not an option.

My sister said, "You're going to take the day off tomorrow, right?" But I didn't do this either.

My best friend kept saying, "And then what happened?" This usually helped, but with each detail, my stomach just churned.

I told my husband, "I don't want to talk anymore." I tried to focus on my *King Lear* paper as the phone rang on, but not one word popped into my head.

Finally, at 2 a.m., I forced myself to go to bed but awoke thrashing and tangled in sheets. Visions of being crushed by angry figures dressed head-to-toe in black still haunted me. They seemed so real I continued flailing my arms and punching at the air.

"Honey, honey—I'm here, you're okay," my husband said, comforting me as I tried to catch my breath.

The next morning on the drive to work, I kept hearing the gunman say, "Where's the key?" as his boots pressed into my sides. When I reached the top of College Avenue, just a block away from the bank, I started to hyperventilate. My face flushed, and tears trickled down my cheeks.

I wanted to go home, but instead, I pulled into the parking lot, counted to ten, and walked into the bank.

All day long, I kept seeing the track star leap the counter. *There he goes again*. Every time someone came into the bank, I looked up, expecting the robbers to storm in and fire bullets into the ceiling, hearing the *pop-pop-pop* again.

At the end of the day, my money drawer was off by $100, something that had not happened since my first week on the job. My supervisor helped me go through all of my transactions, and we realized I had shorted one of my favorite customers. I told myself, *get it together, or you will not be keeping this job.*

After dinner, instead of analyzing *King Lear,* I took out a piece of paper and began to write.

Raw anger poured from my pen: "You advance upon my clothes-pinned torso, to take what is not yours . . ."

I relived the moment, felt the fear well up in me, and let it soak the page: "Slamming sounds spiral closer, breathless black ski masks within reach . . ."

A flicker of electricity sparked up my spine. Air rushed into my lungs as I took a deep breath. It was as if someone else, tall, powerful, was wielding a sword, slicing each detail seared into my brain.

When I was done, it seemed like a poison had been siphoned from a wound deep inside. I felt less heavy and was able to think clearly.

And in this moment, I knew that one day I would write my own stories, each word rising up from the page.

TRIAL AND ERROR

MELISSA JORDAN GREY

I stared at the boysenberry syrup. Preternaturally purple, it clung inside the upside-down bottle and refused to budge despite the smacks of my hand. I held the bottle over my pancakes and waited. Oh, I waited. Free from the controlling, watchful eye of my father, I waited for that syrup to come.

Eating was never joyful in my father's house; it was the Hunger Games of an entirely different sort.

"Do you really want that much spaghetti?" he'd ask at the dinner table.

"What a big serving for such a small girl," he'd say before I'd swallowed my first bite.

To Dad, eating was a test of character. Asking for seconds showed weakness; turning them down showed valor. Eating sugar? God forbid.

But in that downtown Albuquerque IHOP, thousands of miles from home, I waited for that syrup and watched as it rained down in a glorious carbohydrate deluge.

Boysenberry, you're mine.

At sixteen, most girls my age were chasing boys or college dreams. I was sitting across the table from my younger brothers, Matt and Jonny, playing surrogate mother.

None of us uttered a sound. Instead, we focused on the carousel of syrups, the pancakes, the butter—anything but the reason that brought us to this sticky vinyl booth in the first place.

We'd woken up alone that morning in a seedy motel on Central Avenue, home to sex workers, drug peddlers, and an abandoned jailhouse. It was 1983. Unable to afford a safer place, Mom had chosen the Super 8 Motel for its proximity to the Bernalillo County Courthouse, where her second trial against my dad was unfolding.

Just three summers earlier, after our court-mandated visitation with Dad, he and his second wife had decided to send me home early and keep my brothers—permanently. Mom and I found this out the hard way: by waiting at Delta gate 33 until every single passenger had walked off the plane. No Matt, no Jonny. Just Mom and me, standing in shock.

Months later, a judge overturned Dad's attempt to steal the boys. In retaliation, Dad took his ball and went home—withholding child support and leaving Mom to care for three teenagers on nineteen thousand dollars a year. Now, she was in Albuquerque to sue him, and we were there, reluctantly, to testify if called to the stand.

Although we'd been there just ten days, our routine felt oddly familiar. After Mom left early for court each morning, we sat for hours on the musty floral bedspread, watching reruns of *Happy Days*, eating Frosted Flakes out of the ice bucket. Occasionally, out of utter restlessness, Matt slugged Jonny, which offered a noisy respite from the droning TV.

But mostly, we just sat there.

In my unending torpor, I couldn't understand how my father could return me but keep Matt and Jonny. And yet, I understood why. Simply put, I was redundant. Impregnating his secretary while separated from my mother had yielded two slender, graceful daughters who never asked for seconds. Box checked. We all knew this unspoken, painful truth, though my mother had tried to protect me from it.

She couldn't protect me from the Super 8 Motel, though. From the moment the judge had ordered Matt and Jonny home, I'd tried desperately to maintain my parents' fragile cease-fire. At school, I was an overachiever. At home, I cooked, drove the carpool, and did my best to keep Matt and Jonny out of trouble—anything to camouflage our ramshackle, latchkey existence. I didn't want another lawsuit; I wanted a fucking childhood.

My anxiety about the trial intensified the night before we flew to Albuquerque. Dad had called and warned me not to take the stand.

"Don't go, Ellie. Stay the hell out of this, or else. It's got nothing to do with you."

Nothing to do with me? It had everything to do with me. Stealing my brothers, refusing to pay child support, filling our mailbox with endless streams of subpoenas?

And though Dad's foreboding "or else" strangled my breath, Mom shared her own "or else" if I refused: no borrowing the car, no hanging out with my friends—no escape from her daily outbursts.

"You selfish brat!" she'd say. No matter how many times she repeated the phrase, I never felt immune to its sting. And so I went to Albuquerque—hoping to appease Mom, yet terrified that Dad would discover my betrayal.

For as long as my father lived there, I'd hated going to Albuquerque. Its oppressive heat assaulted me outside while my father's disapproval destroyed me from within.

"Don't slouch. Don't be so loud. Don't wear white. It makes you look fat."

Now, as we waited in the hotel room, Jonny leaped incessantly from bed to bed, Matt flipped the channels, and I panicked at the sound of every car—convinced it was Dad coming to get us. To escape, I lay on the bathroom floor, surrounded by faded textbooks, and tried to focus on my schoolwork. The thought of how many days I'd missed made me sick; my precious academic standing imperiled by this bullshit.

And then, suddenly, the phone rang. "Brrrrrrrrring!" I threw down my pencil and bolted out of the bathroom as if that ring was a fire alarm.

Please, please don't let it be him.

Matt shut off the TV, Jonny stopped jumping, and we stood, crippled with fear.

"Brrrrrrrrrrinnnnnng! Brrrrrrrrrrinnnnnng!"

What if it's Dad!? What do we do!?

Cloaked in my big-sister-in-charge façade, I took a deep breath and picked up the phone.

"Hello?"

It wasn't Dad at all. It was Mom with dreaded news.

"It's time to take the stand."

I hung up without uttering a sound. If he didn't know by now, Dad would soon find out we were here.

Hastily, Matt, Jonny, and I put on our "nice clothes" (which, for me, definitely did not include anything white), and I drove to the courthouse in an old station wagon owned by Mom's attorney, Paul T. Wyland, Esq. For years, every time Mom opened mail from "Wyland and Maroni—Attorneys at Law," she exploded in anger—usually hurled in my direction.

"Why can't you help?" she screamed after opening one such letter, pointing at my brothers' dirty dishes, as if their mess had something to do with me.

On the way to the courthouse, Matt and Jonny bickered in a violent kabuki show trapped in the rearview mirror. My head throbbed. Mom met us at the lobby door and ushered us to the top floor to meet the fleshy, middle-aged Mr. Wyland. Still hoping to avoid my dad, I begged, "Can't you do this without me!? I don't want to be here."

Wyland's breath was a malodorous cocktail of stale coffee and Dentyne.

"You don't want to be here?" he said. "I'm missing a Hawaiian vacation for this!"

Asshole.

Moments later, a bailiff summoned us to the courtroom below. As we rushed to the elevator, I felt a fiery bomb explode in my chest. And then, a premonition washed over me with such clarity I couldn't contain it. *Don't take the elevator*, said the voice in my head. *Don't take the elevator.*

"Take the stairs!" I said aloud. "We have to take the stairs! Not the elevator! Please, Mom!! The stairs!!!"

My voice crescendoed but went unheeded.

"WE. HAVE. TO. TAKE. THE. STAIRS!"

But it was too late; we'd already stepped into an open car and begun our descent.

My ribs tightened. Time crawled like boysenberry syrup. And then the doors, like curtains at a magic show, opened to reveal my father towering before us.

Matt, slight in stature, stepped out of the elevator. Immediately, Dad grabbed him and pulled him into the lobby.

"Let him go!" my mom cried, and chased after them.

Paralyzed, I watched as my parents pulled Matt by the arms in a human tug-of-war. Held captive, Matt said nothing. They yanked. They screamed. The cold, hard linoleum floor bounced their shouts like chaotic ping-pong balls.

As Mom clung to Matt, Mr. Wyland tried to free him from my father's grasp. Enraged, Dad retaliated in full force. Within seconds, two grown men in suits swung their fists at one another like adolescents on a sandlot. The soles of their Florsheim oxfords squeaked in protest as their punches soared through the air in slow motion. Every blow hit my nauseated gut. It was a full-blown war.

Through my tears, I looked up to find a swarm of county marshals buzzing the lobby. I shook at the menacing sight of their guns. One of them rushed us outside and then left in an instant, the pain of his grip still pulsing on my shoulder. Matt, Jonny, and I stood on West Washington Street crumpled like the orphaned garbage bags that lined the curb.

I realized I'd gotten my wish. I would not be testifying that day.

War-torn and hungry, Matt, Jonny, and I sought refuge at the International House of Pancakes just miles from the courthouse battleground. We said very little at that table and nothing for years about what had transpired. That's the thing about trauma. It relies on silence to survive.

None of us knew what the next day would bring, but in that tacky little IHOP, I opened my mouth wide and tasted victory—pancakes doused in butter, whipped cream, and boysenberry syrup. Each toothsome bite slid down my throat in a triumphant explosion of freedom. And if only for a moment, life was utterly delicious.

LOVE ON THE BEACH

HEATHER M. BERBERET

There I stood, heart quaking, again on the beach, again waiting to hear my fate. The Oregon dusk gathered misty, wet clouds as the sun sank over the ocean. Despite the rayless light, I could have seen Joan's face clearly if I had dared to look.

I'd crushed on many women over the years, my firsts being the Bionic and the Wonder, falling asleep every night with a superhero doll in my arms. But my fervor evolved when puberty struck in seventh grade, and I passed the torch to an actual person. Her name was Roxanne.

Roxanne exuded a magnetism I associated with superheroes. Sassy, with a touch of butchy spice I still fall for, she'd transfix me the moment our paths crossed in the hallways between the classes. If she tried to chat, my mouth dried into sticky flypaper as I stammered like Bridget Jones.

My starstruck reaction bewildered me. Immersed in immigrant Catholic culture from both sides of my family, growing up in small-town Oregon, the possibility of desiring something other than a friend-ship with a girl *couldn't* occur to me. All I had was my box of superhero feelings, so that's where I dropped Roxanne. Throughout junior high and my freshman year of high school, my unconscious mind worked hard to maintain this state of denial as I "friended" girl after girl, who would then rapidly "unfriend" me when I became "too intense." They joined Roxanne in the box, while I came to believe myself fatalistically weird and out of step with all of teenage-kind.

In October of my high school sophomore year, I met Carole, an artist whose emotional paintings fascinated me. A junior and a Catholic convert, she spoke with more passion about religion than I spoke about *anything*. Like Roxanne, she put on a face of bold independence to distract everyone from her fears of inadequacy. Unlike Roxanne, she pursued *me*, which felt like tumbling into a warm room when someone unexpectedly opened a door against which I'd been huddling during a snowstorm. But, despite declaring ourselves "best friends," I kept space between us, a bit of bubble wrap so that when she left, *it* would pop rather than me.

That spring, Carole and I spent a day at the beach. We argued. She faced me head-on, a brisk wind whipping her frizzy, strawberry-blond hair across her face.

"If you can't promise we'll *always* be best friends, then what's the point of being friends at all?" she asked, her words wobbly.

"I'm your friend now; isn't that enough?" I pleaded, pulled between our separate fears.

"You can't commit to our friendship. That's all I needed to know." She stalked off. I ran after her.

"Fine!" I said. "Fine! I'll be your friend *forever!*"

She turned and wrapped her arms around me in a huge bear hug. We stood there, our backs protecting each other from the wind.

From then on, Carole and I spent hours on the phone. We wrote coded notes and revealed our secrets. I wondered why people valued romantic relationships so much more than friendships. My superhero box no longer seemed ample enough to embrace these feelings, but it was still the only box I had.

As Carole's best friend, I finally belonged, walking with someone until, inevitably, we fell out of step. She stopped writing notes, and then we stopped talking every night on the phone. She became irritated when I waited for her after class, and she told me I needed *other* friends. Carole didn't discard me entirely, but she no longer welcomed me into the inner sanctum of her heart, and she claimed a new girl as her best friend.

It took college and growing up for me to accept that Carole and I subscribed to radically divergent definitions of "forever"; what I wanted from our friendship, what I believed we promised each other, I wasn't going to get.

The loneliness I took for granted before Carole grew more intense after her, and my belief that I marched out of cadence with everyone else's drum grew stronger than ever.

Until I met Joan.

Joan shared a similar charismatic personality with Carole, but she was funny, really funny, with such a wacky sense of humor that I called her "Muppet." She had a knack for finding the faintest beam of light in the darkness. She valued helping others above everything else. A volunteer at the local peace-and-justice community, Joan gave it her all, whether serving food at the soup kitchen or covering a vacant overnight shift at the halfway house at the last minute.

Mostly, she made me laugh.

Volunteering together built trust between us. Eventually, we started hanging out socially, became friends, and got real. We revealed our past dramas and came to depend on each other to get through the current ones. One night, late and alone in her apartment, she told me about falling in love with a woman in high school. "A fluke," she said, "which doesn't mean I'm gay." That didn't have anything to do with me or my feelings, but like a melody stuck in my mind, I just couldn't leave it alone.

After I graduated, Joan and I took a vacation to Oregon. Without a plan and with a rental car entirely at our disposal, we reveled in the freedom. Our final day was spent at the coast. I had a phone session in the afternoon with my therapist, Elaine.

"I fought with Mom before we left," I told her. "She said if I didn't get a job soon, I'd spend the rest of my life flipping burgers. How could she say that? Afterward, I lost it. I know I shouldn't have, but I asked Joan to hold me again," I said quickly, all in one breath.

Elaine paused. "You know, you talk about Joan like you would talk about a lover."

Silence. The silence that truth makes when it crashes over you in a tidal wave of connected dots and realizations.

Yep. *That's* how I felt about Joan, and Carole, and Roxanne, and all the others.

Many people experience torturous coming-out stories. While I would one day garner my fair share of gay tragedy, at that moment, I felt glorious relief, a lightening of being—satisfaction like the swoosh of a basketball dropping through the net without touching the rim. Falling in love with Joan and all the girls before her—those strange, inappropriate, idiosyncratic feelings were, in fact, perfectly normal. Finally, I had a box that fit all of them and all of me.

"You're right," I told Elaine. "That *is* who I am."

I loved Joan. I wanted to be with Joan. But Joan swore she was straight. Would our friendship be sustained if I declared my feelings and she didn't love me in return? But if I didn't tell her, would I crumble back into my personal well of loneliness, out of sync forever?

In the end, gay or straight, I am who I am—a big blabbermouth.

My session ended, and heart hammering, I made my way back to the beach where Joan waited for me. I paced back and forth across the cold sand as the golden sunshine melted into a gray, nebulous twilight.

"I have to tell you something," I said again, repeating myself for the tenth time.

"Yes, you mentioned that. Just say it. How bad can it be?" Joan replied.

"If I tell you, it'll be so weird. We'll stop being friends."

She stood up from the mammoth driftwood log upon which she had been patiently watching me freak out, put her hands on my shoulders, and looked deeply into my eyes. "Tell me," she commanded.

I started crying, breaking the terrible tension between holding onto her and holding onto me. I dropped my face into my hands, because looking at her when I said this seemed more than I could endure.

"My feelings have pushed so many people away. But I can't hide, I can't *not* tell you . . ." I mumbled through my fingers. Then, the words pushed out, tumbling over each other like water over rocks. "I love you. I love you more than friendship. I mean, I *love you,* love you. And you can feel how you feel. We can feel different things. I get it that you don't feel that way about me. It's OK."

I held my breath, blood roaring in my ears, hunching my shoulders as if to protect myself from a blow, and waited. Her hands touched mine, encouraging me to lower them. Stiffening my arms, I resisted a little, but I couldn't stand on the beach covering my face for the rest of my life, so I laughed as I cried and gave in. One of her hands held onto mine, but the other let go. I felt it under my chin, asking me to look up—to look at her.

She smiled with her mouth and her brows, lifting her entire face. Her blue eyes focused on mine. At the time, I told myself the wind made them water, but I wonder now if she wasn't crying with me.

"See," she said. "I'm still here."

LIFE AFTER DEATH

LORI TULLIS

"Something is wrong with me, Jordan," I cried, as my twenty-seven-year-old son opened his front door, surprised to see me on his doorstep.

For eight weeks, I had been faced with nothing but questions. Why hadn't I been sleeping well? Why was I so tired? Why was I always gasping for breath? I had still managed my work as a caregiver, but my breathing was different that morning. I hadn't slept in twenty-four hours and could feel a tightening in my chest. I called in sick to work—something I never did. I couldn't put words to it, but on that beautiful, bright, snowy March day in Bend, Oregon, I knew I needed help.

Jordan welcomed me into his house. He looked at me with worry in his eyes. I tried to reassure him. "I may need to go to the doctor, but right now, I just want to be with you and get some sleep. If I'm not better by tomorrow, I'll go."

His green eyes shined with loving reassurance. "Mom, just stay with me until we get this figured out." Jordan and I spent the day together. I was able to take a fitful nap, though my head still swirled with questions. After a quiet evening, I headed into his spare bedroom, hoping a night's sleep would cure me. Instead, every time I dozed off, I awoke with a startle, fighting to breathe. Unbeknownst to me, my lungs were filling with fluid. At about 3 a.m., I sat up in bed and threw up. Jordan took one look at me and announced we were going to the doctor.

We arrived at urgent care the minute it opened that morning. The petite blond doctor looked at me with concern. "You need to go to the

71

hospital right now. Your heart is in a chaotic rhythm." I fell back into a swirl of questions. Ever since I was a teenager, I routinely had tachycardia (a rapid heartbeat) and atrial fibrillation (an irregular heartbeat), and this morning I was having both? I had always been told the issues were minor. So, what was really going on? What was making me feel so sick?

Jordan drove me straight to the hospital. At 9 a.m., I was placed in one of the private ER rooms. A few hours later, a middle-aged cardiologist entered the room. I could barely meet his eyes. He spoke words I was not at all prepared to hear. "You're in heart failure and need open heart surgery to replace your mitral valve as soon as possible."

I was in a state of shock, too frozen to comprehend what the doctor was saying. I was a vegan, didn't drink or smoke, and rarely took over-the-counter meds. I lived in the mountains, breathing fresh air and drinking purified water, so the diagnosis felt like a cruel joke. Yet now, all the symptoms made sense. Being unable to sleep. Unable to catch my breath. But open heart surgery? The news brought me back to thoughts of my childhood, one where I felt I never quite belonged, one where I wondered why I had been brought to this earth.

***

It was July and a picture-perfect Oregon day. I was still recovering at Jordan's but felt my energy returning. Could this nightmare be over? It was as if I had been stuck in an endless tunnel of thunderstorms for months, and now the sunshine had finally come out. I had so much energy, I decided to mow his lawn and put on my bathing suit to soak up some vitamin D in the backyard. Jordan had lost electricity at his work site, so he came home. Later that afternoon, I suggested, "Let's just drive over to the site and see if the electricity is back on."

At 2:45 p.m., we walked out to the car, and he got into the driver's side—which I remember thinking was odd, because he hardly ever drives. We had just turned right onto Portland Avenue in the north part of town, and as we passed over the Deschutes River, I marveled at its beauty. The way the water flowed.

Time slowed.

Out of nowhere, I felt a sudden rush of emotion.

Tears formed. And fell.

I turned to Jordan. "Thank you for everything you've done for me over the past eight weeks. I love you so much," and then, apparently, my head dropped onto my chest. Darkness.

***

Jordan later told me all the things that happened next. When he saw me slumped over in the passenger seat, he quickly pulled the car into a residential area. Panicked, he checked my wrists and realized I didn't have a pulse. He wondered if I had died. He ran to the passenger side and pulled me onto the grassy area between the road and a sidewalk. He tried to call 911 but couldn't maintain a connection. He ran into the street and looked at everyone passing with a silent scream that said, "Help me!" He rushed back to where I was lying on the ground. With a silent prayer, he placed his hands on my chest as he tried to perform CPR.

There was no heartbeat.

A small crowd surrounded us, watching and waiting. Wondering if I would live. He could feel my ribs breaking but continued with CPR. One beautiful young girl with long, wavy blond hair and a face full of freckles asked, "What can I do?"

"Get 911 on the phone," Jordan yelled, while still pumping my chest. The crowd grew. There were now maybe forty people. They watched as a police officer rode up on his motorcycle, jumped off, grabbed some gloves, and took over CPR.

They watched as a tall, slender man with salt-and-pepper hair said to the police officer, "You need to place your hands higher and pump a little faster." "Mind your own business!" the officer had yelled back, not knowing that the man was a doctor. The policeman did what the doctor said, but still, there was no heartbeat. The crowd watched as the paramedics arrived and rushed over. They cut open my Ganesha T-shirt and my bra and applied the paddles. And finally, a heartbeat.

But again it was fatal, beating at about 400 beats per minute. The crowd watched as I was placed into the ambulance and rushed to the hospital. Jordan was there to see that I had to be shocked multiple times in the ER to keep my heart going.

The next day, I lay in my hospital bed, a total blank. I remembered nothing. I came in and out of consciousness. The nurses explained that I most likely had post-traumatic amnesia. When I felt more conscious, they explained the story once more. There had been no heartbeat for six to eight minutes. I had died or nearly died.

As someone who knew quite a bit about others' near-death experiences, I wondered why I couldn't remember. Others had reported having visions, or calming or miraculous experiences. But I was a blank. Left again with only questions. Where was I when my heart stopped? Was I floating above the scene? Did I leave the side of the road and traverse other realms? Who was I face-to-face with, in the ethers, while my heart was pounding so hard? Questions again swirled.

***

Years later, while in a hypnotherapy session, a flicker of remembrance entered my mind—it was as if I was right back on the ground when my heart had stopped, only this time I floated upward. I saw a door in the sky with golden light shining around the edges. As I entered, I felt a sense of home, a sense of being connected to every being on the planet.

I understood my role.

I felt loved—unconditionally.

I understood there was no longer a need for questions.

When I woke from this vision, I knew I was forever changed. Instead of a head swirling with "why" questions, my whole being had been calmed with waves of acceptance. Why I had been placed on earth was unfolding at the pace it was supposed to unfold. I was loved and was free to love. I thought back on my son and how he rushed to help me that day when my head fell to my chest. I felt his overwhelming love for me, wanting me to survive. I knew that from that day forward, no matter if my experiences were good or bad, I would forever be able to live in the compassion I was shown on that day by the river.

LOVE YOU, PA X

LAUREN CROSS

The summer after I miscarried, a purple hummingbird would visit me. I would sit at my computer by a window, tapping out my grief. One cooler afternoon, I opened the window to enjoy the warm breeze, carrying aloft the amber-vanilla scent of rock roses, when I heard a loud buzzing. I looked up, thinking it must be a large bee or a flying beetle. But it was another creature watching me. It turned its head to look at me, beady bird eye to beady human eye, showing off its magenta feathers with viridian under-plumage. It moved how you might imagine a feathered alien spaceship would move—erratically hovering as it studies human life before zooming off at an unexpected angle in a flash of iridescent purple. Day after day, the little bird would visit. The tiniest of creatures manifesting the tiniest of babies lost. *Is that you, Bean?*

There were also signs of an afterlife in the wintery days after my dog died. My brooch with prancing greyhounds mysteriously unpinned itself from my cardigan and clung, like static, to my toddler's pajamas. The next morning, a dog face with a cocked ear appeared in the condensation of the window above where he used to sleep. A brown hummingbird swooped and squeaked above my head the following week when I collected my dog's ashes from the vet.

And more than half a lifetime ago, after my beloved great-grand-mother died, I saw a diffuse light at the end of my bed. That night, I dreamt of her. *I love you, I love you, I'll always be with you.* It was a hug from across the great beyond.

But, my dearest Pa, why have you not given me such concrete signs? How is it that my baby, my dog, and my great-grandmother could find me, but you who loved me all of my life, you who are one-half of the reason for my existence, cannot? Your silence makes me question all previous supernatural experiences. How do I know what is real and what is not? Now that I am forever chasing after three children who scale and scramble over things they shouldn't—a different heart-stopping relationship—maybe I haven't been paying close enough attention.

Is it you who visits me while I sleep, or is my brain conjuring your memory to propel me forward in healing? I look for messages from you in the swill of tea leaves at the bottom of my mug. Sometimes, I fancy there's a whisper of smoke and cedar—your smell. At other times—a song playing, a breeze ruffling my hair—I wonder if it's your ghost passing through me. I look for you in my backyard. Are you the dragonfly that landed near me in the hours after your death? Or one of the hummingbirds that nest in the red pepper tree?

Even if these are signs from you, it is not you. It seems impossible that you're gone. Impossible, until it hits me: that loving, maddening, complicated, playful, fiery man that is—*was*—you, my dad, is gone. All that experience gone. The stories, the music, gone.

Tangible traces of you may exist in your house 6,000 miles away, but here in California, the only thing I have to hold onto is your love. On the advice of a grief counselor, I must find a new way to have a relationship with you in death. This feels almost ridiculous, until I read all the letters you ever sent me, dating back to when I was a young girl. They all say the same thing: *I love you, I miss you, I want the best for you, I am proud of you, I will love you until the day I die.*

I think you still love me, somehow. I don't feel less loved now that you're dead, but there is a hollowness. Like an egg without salt, love without my dad radiating it satiates hunger but lacks flavor. It is nourishment without the pleasure, but there is a bland comfort that sustains me.

Sometimes I log in to your email account and toggle to your drafts folder. There is just one unsent email, empty, save for my address in the To line. You started it two hours before you died. I'll always wonder what you wanted to say.

I imagine: *Hello love, I am dying. Now I am scared, but I don't want you to worry. Remember the song I wrote you: I have loved you all your life, I am always by your side, and ever shall I stay. Kiss those babies for me. This is not goodbye. Love you, PAX.*

You would have signed your name, Pa, with an 'x' for a kiss, in all caps, the way all of your letters in recent decades did. I always wondered if it was an unspoken but deliberate Latin contraction for the state of tranquility you were forever chasing: *PA X, pax, peace.*

I seek out new rituals to nurture my new relationship with you. On the upcoming one-year anniversary of your death, I will still be trapped on the other side of the world by the pandemic, still unable to mourn you alongside family. You have long been returned to Stardust, and I still haven't been hugged by my mum or brother. To literally and figuratively mark the first anniversary of your death, I will get my first tattoo: LOVE PAX in your handwriting.

I write you letters after the kids are in bed. There have been drunken missives and sober thoughts as I tap out a new grief. My six-year-old, the only grandchild you ever really got to know, sometimes sees me crying. She's learned that drawing a picture of you with the letters P-A-X makes me smile again. She knows that grief must be held tenderly, sometimes by a drawing of hands signing *not okay* in ASL. Her words make my hand cover my heart: "You're crying because you miss your dad, Mom? But he's still your dad, and he's still my grandpa. He still loves us, and we still love him. It's just different."

I show family photos to my two younger children. "Who's that? Who's that?" I ask, pointing at faces. When we reach the photo of you, they squeal, "Gampa Darling!" As toddlers, they are too young to remember you, but somehow they know who you are anyway. You are gone but not forgotten. And I am waiting.

ANDY WARHOL IS DEAD AND I'M SOBER

ROBERT KIRK

I've been sober for about nine months. I don't wake up hungover with my brain pounding against my skull anymore. I don't get warning letters from the dorm manager telling me I'm about to get kicked out, and I never hear people in class saying, "Wow, you sure were drunk last night."

I never knew what "you sure were drunk last night" meant. Did it mean I'd tried to make out with the person? Did it mean I'd puked or peed on their floor? Who could know?

Even though life is way better now, if I'm being honest, I miss the party. That was my identity. I was the party guy.

Here's the thing: I'm twenty years old. I've never even had a legal drink. How can I be burned out already?

Yes, I need to be sober. Of course I do. But sometimes, it's like I'm living in this endless stream of predictability. I seem to have all these new recovery-program rules to follow.

I know I can't party like a normal college guy. I get it. Every time I do, things explode into chaos, like fights, random sex, or blackouts. Once, I even woke up with a knife next to my bed and had to check it for blood, wondering if maybe I'd stabbed this annoying, born-again fundamentalist guy from the seventh floor. I hadn't.

Everything is better now. I have a sponsor. I'm doing well at school and have a cool internship with a TV show at ABC. I never could have pulled that off before sobriety. And yet this frustration, this gnawing feeling that I'd left excitement behind, with no adventures ahead of me, came to a head a few nights ago.

Here's what happened: I was with a couple of friends from the dorm, and we watched *The Doors*, that Oliver Stone movie—massive mistake. There's a scene with Andy Warhol, and that scene is all I've been thinking about. The band goes to Andy Warhol's Factory after their New York show, and the regulars at the Factory are so whacked that even the Doors get freaked out. Seriously, Andy Warhol's party is too much for the Doors. But before they leave, Andy gives Jim Morrison this golden telephone and tells him he can use it to call God. I wanted to jump into the movie. I wanted to be cool enough to call God and freak out the Doors.

Instead, it's late at night in New York City and I'm downstairs in the dorm basement doing laundry, watching my clothes spin around in the dryer. This new sober life is definitely too sedate for Andy Warhol's crowd.

I've seen all the Warhol documentaries. I know all his supporting characters. The famous artists in his orbit were edgy, unpredictable. My high school dream was to leave San Diego and find Andy Warhol. In this fantasy, he'd have invited drug-addled me into his inner world like a superstar. I'd have partied all night, lounging around the Factory intoxicated, just like the real inner-circle characters I'd read about. But that never happened. I'm away at college, finally living in Manhattan, but Andy Warhol is dead, and I'm sober.

This whole thing just isn't going according to plan.

I need to go over the edge one more time to prove to myself that my life hasn't already morphed into a state of middle-aged boredom. I need a blast of something wild.

I know where the parties are. I could easily go get trashed one last time.

But I can't drink or take drugs. I really can't.

Fuck.

I call my friend Matthew from AA. Matthew is older than me, obviously. Everyone in AA is older than me. But he's cool, in his late twenties, and works at MTV. Recently, he hung out with Whitney Houston as her personal escort for the day, which is very New York.

"I'm in a rut," I say to him on the phone. "I do the same thing every night."

"I get it," he says. "Come to my place tomorrow night. We can go to this little meeting in Soho that I think you'll like. Shake up your routine a little."

Another AA meeting? Not exactly the jolt of adventure I'm looking for. But okay. Whatever.

The next night, Matthew and I take a taxi to this warehouse-type building in Soho with a metal industrial elevator like the one Glenn Close and Michael Douglas rode in *Fatal Attraction*.

"It's a Big Book study," Matthew says, as the elevator clunks its way upstairs. "A small meeting."

Thrilling.

On the third floor, we walk into this drab, fluorescent-lit room that smells like coffee and cigarettes. A couple of long card tables are in the middle of the room, surrounded by metal folding chairs. Matthew finds us seats while I grab a Styrofoam cup of coffee with powdered creamer. Everyone in the room is quiet and looks older than my parents. I sit next to Matthew and take a sip of the warmish coffee, swallowing an undissolved clump of cream. I close my eyes for a minute, yawn, and vow not to fall asleep.

I open my eyes, doing my best to pay attention.

That's when I look across the table, and it happens.

Holy fuck.

I kid you not.

Sitting directly across from me at this very same table is one of Andy Warhol's top artists. And this guy is no minor character. He's one of those inner-sanctum characters I've seen in all the Warhol documentaries and books. He's closer to my dad's age than my age now, but without question, it's him.

Be chill. We're in an AA meeting.

Wait! He isn't drugged up at a party. He's at a meeting. This guy who lived the life I wanted to live is sober and at a meeting, just like me.

This guy in front of me has been deep inside that world that freaked out the Doors.

I play it smooth and just kick back in my chair as some lady drones on about the Big Book.

The meeting comes to an end, and I'm not exactly sure what to do. I want to jump all over the artist and ask for stories. But I also don't want to act weird. I know that would be weird.

Matthew comes to the rescue.

"Have you met my friend Robb?" he says to the artist.

"No, I don't think I have," the artist says.

Then, this woman comes over from the other table and puts her hand on the artist's shoulder. Her skin is flawless, her lips smile red, and she's so tall, her legs look like stilts.

"Lydia and I are walking over to the San Genaro festival in Little Italy," the artist says. "Do you guys want to come along?"

"I don't know," Matthew says. "What do you think about that idea, Robb?"

"That sounds good," I say, going for a low-key, unimpressed vibe of *Sure, I can go to a New York street festival with one of Warhol's top artists tonight.*

As we're waiting for them over by the door, Matthew softly says, "He used to work for Andy Warhol."

"Yes, of course, I know that," I say.

"And Lydia is a bit of a celebrity, too, in certain adult-entertainment venues. They've both been sober forever."

Lydia and the artist come over to us.

"Ready?" the artist says.

Lydia takes my arm, and the four of us head to the elevator.

As we walk along the nighttime streets of New York, the artist seems to know everyone in Lower Manhattan. He's a downtown star, and I'm standing next to him the whole time like an old pal. The four of us push through crowds, eat pizza from a food truck, and ride a Ferris wheel installed in a narrow city street for the carnival.

I hear about Lydia's work dancing naked on stage and how the artist was with Andy when he snapped some of the now-famous Polaroids.

They both tell me over and over how grateful they are to be sober. These are AA old-timers.

They show me how we can do whatever we want in sobriety. There are no rules. This isn't church. Sobriety just levels the playing field, so we have a shot at our dreams. I mean, I can be edgy or sedate, whatever suits the moment. I can do anything I want, as long as I do it without using alcohol or drugs.

***

It's been almost thirty-three years since that night. I've partied sober in the big clubs of Fire Island, London, and New York. I've expanded my ideas of adventure and worked in bookstores and museums, drinking literature and art into my soul. I've filled up stacks of journals, writing at the street cafes of Paris, inside the Pyramids of Egypt, on the islands of Greece. It's all been grounded in sobriety. Once, I even whipped up an AA meeting with a few other Americans as we zipped across China on a train. Instead of getting high and imagining an exciting life, I've stayed sober and actually lived one.

NOT-SO-SACRA-CONVERSAZIONE

MARILYN WOODS

All my life, I've worried: *too* tall, *too* loud, *too* much of a tomboy. *Too* drunk, *too* disrespectful, *too* prissy. *Too* flirty, *too* flighty, *too* many freckles. *Too* uppity, *too* mundane, *too* many speeding tickets. *Too* weak, *too* strong, *too* scattered. *Too* fat, *too* flabby, *too* athletic. *Too* much shit to worry about.

And now, when I've pretty much got a handle on it all, *too* old rears its ugly head.

People like me are often referred to as old, over-the-hill, aged, ancient, and the worst of all—elderly. What the fuck is elderly? What's the start date? I assume it lasts until you die. Recently, I heard on NPR that if a woman's mom lives into her nineties, the woman has a strong propensity to follow suit. My flirtatious and glamorous mother sizzled well into her eighties and lived to be ninety-four.

Perhaps I should stop being *too* anxious and embrace my role as an elder as something beyond the denotation of chronological age. Elder: a person of authority because of age and experience. Should I share the richness of my life experience? Is it time for me to stop resisting my station in life and find a way to enrich the lives of those around me?

As I searched for answers, a friend advised, "Read Cicero." She meant Marcus Tullius Cicero, now just Cicero. One-name fame long before Cher or Beyoncé. It didn't take long to see that the great Roman orator and statesman, born in 106 BC, had a handle on my frustration. Cicero was one of the most prolific Roman writers, and his letters, treatises, speeches, and books have survived into the modern era. We authors gotta hang together.

In one sitting, I devoured the small volume *How to Grow Old: Ancient Wisdom for the Second Half of Life*. As I closed the cover, I found myself desperately wanting to talk to the guy. I needed his wisdom, and soon I imagined the two of us in a secular kind of *sacra conversazione*. After all, the "holy conversation" concept—usually the Virgin and Child with Saints—originated in Italy, Cicero's home, in the first half of the fifteenth century. Ours would be a secular conversation—no Jesus, no Madonna, no Anthony, Paul, or John—just the two of us. A dialogue.

I plopped down in my daydream chair and began to imagine the two of us together in my garden.

"Come sit here, Mr. Cicero," I invited, extending my right arm with palm open as I recalled his gesture memorialized in the marble statue of the great orator in front of the Palace of Justice in Rome. It was happening.

His handsomeness startled me. Oh, I realized this is where "chiseled" came from, as I surveyed his angular face with a strong jaw, a broad forehead, and an aquiline nose. People with Roman noses are said to have excellent leadership skills and strong personalities.

He, Cicero, wore the defining Roman garment, the toga. Its chalk-white color highlighted his flawless god-like bronzed complexion. I took care not to stare as he settled on the bench in my walled garden, which flourished with mingled scents of lavender and rosemary. With care, he closed the toga's opening. I breathed a sigh of relief, aware that, most likely underneath, he wore nothing but a loincloth. In an attempt to curtail my nerves, I remained standing, ramrod stiff, overflowing with awkwardness. I waited.

My already uncontrollable nervous condition heightened when he patted his sculptured hand on the bench's empty spot next to him. I inhaled deeply and complied. "Thank you, Mr. Cicero," I murmured to Rome's greatest orator, philosopher, verse writer, and influential statesman, who just happened to inspire my country's Founding Fathers and Winston Churchill. Here was my opportunity to have my thinking set on a new path. After inhaling and exhaling to the point of near fainting, I addressed my guest. "You see, I purchased your book on growing old because I'm concerned about the concept of aging." I shifted and added, "Being elderly."

As I spoke, he patted my hand, ignoring the brown spots. I paused, hoping here, next to me in my garden, he would be inclined to defend old age against its disadvantages, mine in particular, as he had in his writings. Instead, he encouraged me to expound. I spewed, "I always loved to play tennis and ski, snow and water! Now, I'm lucky if I finish a three-mile power walk . . . I have no romance in my life . . . uh . . . younger people ignore me and—"

Again touching my hand, he interrupted. "Why don't you slow down just a bit . . . ?"

More blathering. "I don't want to die. I just want to have some fun."

At this point, he stood to face me, toga securely wrapped. He turned his head toward the sunlight, both arms outstretched as if to orate. *That's what he does, right?* I thought. What followed played out more like counseling from a good friend, as Gail often does.

"It's true that aging withdraws from active pursuits . . . and secondly, the body does get weaker."

He philosophized. Please don't let him stop. This couldn't be happening. He was on a roll. I particularly liked his aside, "I don't care for the word *elderly* either, hence the substituted *old age* in my writings."

His wisdom enthralled me. He mustn't leave, I told myself. We needed a break. Ice-cold lemonade. A cookie. If I went to the kitchen, would he leave? Maybe he'd stay longer. I took the chance and was delighted over his "Thank you very much. Quite refreshing.

"Nature will always win," he continued, after a toga adjustment.

"Certain things, like your more rigorous physical activities, are meant to be enjoyed at different times of life, not now. Trying to cling to youthful activities in old age will lead to frustration and resentment. But rejoice that you were an active youth—that's why you're in such lovely shape now." And then, with a sweet smile, he leaned toward me and whispered, "Don't you like to dance? Slow dance?"

I felt myself flush scarlet, perhaps because I sensed what came next. He's gonna get to the sex stuff; I steeled myself. Sure enough, back in our sacra less-than-holy conversazione, my now friend, the philosopher, broached it. "About your romantic life . . ."

He paused, taking note of my squirming. "Yes, as older folks, we are deprived of almost all physical, sensual pleasures. But not all," he said, as he brushed his shoulder against mine.

Just how old is he? I wondered. And then aloud, with surprising courage, "What's a girl to do, Mr. Cicero? I have a very good memory, and there's a lot of action I miss."

I felt my head rotate swiftly away from his gaze. He waited for my head to slowly shift back and he counseled, "Where lust rules, there is no place for self-control."

Maybe not like a therapist, but more like a reprimand from a strict parent or teacher. He began marching toward his big finish—standing not behind a podium but right here with me. "You, I can imagine, were active and full of energy in your younger days, right? Even today, I note you have a real bounce in your step. Exercise, moderation in food and drink, and care for your intellect. You do all that, don't you?"

I muttered an inane response, barely audible. He continued realigning my thinking. "Life's racecourse is fixed, you see. Nature has only a single path, and that path is run but once, and to each stage of existence has been allotted its own appropriate quality; so that the weakness of childhood, the impetuosity of youth, the seriousness of middle life, the maturity of old age—each bear some of Nature's fruit, which must be garnered in its own season."

"I am a very ripe old peach," my unspoken response. I gulped my lemonade; he took a measured sip. And then, almost verbatim from my favorite part of his book, he went on, "You know, old age has no extravagant banquets, no tables piled high, no wine cups filled again and again, but it also has no drunkenness, no indignation, and no sleepless nights."

I have a very good imagination, and at this point, a stirring arose in me as Michael Bublé began to sing from my balcony. I would run with it.

Cicero stood, held out his hand, and took me in his arms in a slow dance. With the last twirl, he escorted me back to the bench and lowered himself next to me. I melted into his final words of wisdom, "I know no reason old age should be lacking in gratification."

Aware of my slowly beating heart, I stayed in my reverie for a long while. As the sun began its slow descent, Mr. Cicero left me to my thoughts. I ruminated about my love of nature and gardening being stronger than ever now. Cicero encouraged it as a worthwhile pursuit in old age. "The good fortune of growing things is something every old person can enjoy. The cultivation of the soil is something we can pursue even to the end of our days."

At sunset, in this remarkable moment, at my age, in my garden, I lingered. *Too* contented.

PENSACOLA 1969

STEPHEN SCHROETER

I wake up and touch my head, which is shaved and sunburned. I pull on an old flight suit and head out to march on the grinder as I try to follow the barked and barely comprehensible commands of our Marine drill instructor. If you fall out of step, you get a sharp slap on the side of your head and then have to do squat thrusts in the 100-degree Florida heat, which could result in spending time in the base hospital.

I alert my ears to the sounds of slaps and grunts, hoping I won't be the next victim. It is 1969, the height of the Vietnam War, and like a good boy, I followed my father and grandfather and joined the Navy. I loved the physical stresses of Marine boot camp and being part of a team. It was like my college fraternity rushes at UCLA. I was training to be a flight weapons officer, who, once commissioned, would sit in the backseat of an F-4 Phantom and rain destruction on the enemy.

I'm in line at the mess hall with my tray when I see two of my instructors talking. They are young naval officers who have just returned from a tour in Vietnam. I crane my neck and hear one say, "What we're doing over there is wrong, but we all have a duty as officers and gentlemen to carry on." The other one nods. That afternoon, we officer candidates sit in neat rows in a large military auditorium. An admiral in a freshly pressed uniform shining with medals is there to make a motivational presentation called the Admiral's Mast. To get us revved up. To encourage us to be the best soldiers we can be. He growls with pride, "We got those fucking gooks. They were

89

on the Ho Chi Minh Trail, bringing weapons and supplies by bicycle to the Vietcong. So we strafed them."

Later that night, I'm sitting in our sparse barracks with my four buddies, watching the news on our small black-and-white television. We had heard about the My Lai massacre, when the US Army murdered more than four hundred unarmed civilians in a small province in the So'n Tinh district of South Vietnam. And now, the grim reporter is playing new horrific footage, videos of napalmed women and children running naked through the streets of Vietnam. I am frozen in my chair, a knot growing in my stomach. The enormity of what we are doing there begins to sink into my brain. I feel as if a fog is lifting. A few recruits mutter, "This is so fucked up." Others brush it off. All I can think is, *What are we doing over there?*

The next day, an officer gives a talk on how to keep our uniforms neat, the proper behavior of Navy wives, and the honor system. He admires how he looks in his dress whites and then says, "The Navy is superior to the Air Force because of our honor system. See, the Air Force pilots operate on a point system, while Navy pilots have a fixed deployment. Air Force pilots get a certain number of points for flying over enemy territory, a certain number of points for dropping ordnance, and a certain number of points for a hit. All of these points are verified by reconnaissance aircraft that accompany the bombers. One time, this Air Force guy, in order to get enough points to end a deployment and go home, simply dropped his bombs without thinking about the consequences and obliterated a village, likely killing women and children."

I feel myself pulling away from the world around me. Everything grows silent. Thoughts race through my head. What am I going to do? Can I really be a part of this? Everything I've been told is not true. We are the murderers. The uniform I am wearing feels like a joke.

Another training officer takes to the podium and tells a war story that makes us look at our place in the war from the viewpoint of civilians. "A Navy squadron with bombers and recon planes flew over enemy territory, and the lead plane in the squadron was shot down. The pilot ejected successfully; however, when the recon plane circled, they saw that the pilot had been decapitated and his head had been placed in the middle of his parachute." Our instructor looks at us to make sure we get the lesson. "Listen to me. If and when you are ever shot down, avoid the civilian villagers at all costs. Why? Well, if someone were dropping shit on you, killing your family members, of course, you would want to kill them. And you would be right in doing so. You don't have a moral leg to stand on. But this is what you're signing up for, boys." Then he shrugs and leaves the podium.

After that lecture, I walk with my buddies to see a movie on base. *Lonely Are the Brave*, starring Kirk Douglas as Sandy, a rugged individualist who didn't heed social causes but had a clear sense of honor. His brother-in-law was an immigration activist willing to stand up for what he thought was right, and as a result, got jailed for helping Mexican immigrants. Both characters end up in the same cell. Sandy sawed through the bars with a hacksaw that he had smuggled in. He was going to escape, but his more principled brother-in-law refused to join him and decided to face the injustice and stay in jail for his cause. Sandy escaped and fled to the border on his faithful horse but was struck by a truck as he crossed a road. His horse died, and Sandy was injured and returned to jail. This is when I know I have to stand my ground and do the right thing, just like Sandy's brother-in-law.

I had never been one to rock the boat and was certainly not an anti-war activist before I joined the Navy, but as I lie in my bunk that night, images from the movie and of napalmed women and decapitated men circle in my brain. I can hear the admiral say, "We all have a job to do defending the US, and it's our patriotic duty to do it!"

As I close my eyes, I see the face of Sandy's brother-in-law in *Lonely Are the Brave*, willing to face the consequences to honor his cause. For the first night in weeks, I sleep soundly. The next day, I wake up with a sense of resolve and march up to my lieutenant. "I want to DOR," a Drop on Request, which means I want out. I set my jaw, knowing that no matter what he says, I will follow through and refuse my commission. He looks up. A flash of fear washes through me, and I brace myself. He, with some sympathy in his eyes, says, "What? Why do you want to do this?"

"I can't support this war."

He asks, "Are the war stories bothering you?"

"Yes, they are," I say. "Are they true?"

"Yes, they're true, but that is war, and we have a duty to serve." He looks hard at me and says, "So you are really going to quit?"

I lift my chin and tighten it to stand firm. "Yes."

He shakes his head. "That just means somebody else has to go in your place."

I look him in the eyes and say, "They can make the same decision I've made not to go."

Over the next several months, I am interviewed up the chain of command. The further I get up the line, the more critical the officers become. I am called an unpatriotic coward and a shirker. When I get all the way up to the admiral, I'm afraid I'll be put in the brig. I explain my reasons for refusing and brace myself. My eyes widen in surprise, as he is sympathetic.

"Well, I don't agree with it, but I respect your decision."

I sign papers to refuse my commission. Had I been an enlisted man, I almost certainly would be court-martialed, serve time, and be dishonorably discharged. An officer candidate gets an honorable discharge.

I am in a kind of limbo while they process my case. I am put in an area called Battalion X, where I scrape the bottom of boats all day. I am in a new group with other "bad influencers." They segregate us so we will not affect the other officer candidates with our subversive views of the war.

One night, I look out the window to see strong winds blowing palm trees, and then I hear a screeching alarm from a tall tower outside. Windows are being boarded up to withstand the power of Hurricane Camille. I lie back on my bunk with my arms behind my head, look up at the ceiling, and take a long breath, resolute in my decision, feeling calm in the eye of the storm.

POSTPARTUM WORK

SHARON ROSEN LEIB

The criminal defendant I prosecuted just before giving birth to my first child repeatedly and violently shook a baby in her care to death. The jury convicted her of manslaughter. That case messed with my mind. How could a caregiver kill the baby she was hired to protect?

No wonder I was paranoid and depressed—looking at every child-care provider as a potential killer made my returning to work as a deputy attorney general seem like being an accessory to a crime.

Even when our baby started sleeping through the night, I didn't. I couldn't focus enough to read a book or carry on a conversation with my husband. My descent into psychosis two years prior primed him to see the signs of disintegration. When baby Hannah hit the four-month mark, I blankly gazed at the three bridges outside our Berkeley window (the Bay, Golden Gate, and Richmond-San Rafael) and dutifully nursed like a prized milk cow. I teetered on the brink of falling into a bridgeless void.

One warm Friday evening in July of 1994, my husband came home to discover me on the sofa gazing at the bridges with my boobs out, the baby asleep on my lap, and the TV droning.

"How long have you been sitting like that?" he asked.

"No idea." I didn't bother rotating my head to look at him.

My blankness spooked him. "I think you should make an appointment with the psychiatrist. Maybe you need to go back on your medication," he said. That caught my attention. I knew I was depressed, but was I that bad off? I turned my head to look at him.

"If I go back on medication, I'll have to stop nursing."

"You've nursed long enough. You need to take care of yourself now. And maybe you should go back to work part-time," he said.

"Really? You think it's time?"

"Definitely. You'll lose it if you just sit here by yourself all day. I would."

His empathy perked me up. He was giving the cow a prod and permission to leave the barn.

"Okay. I'll call tomorrow. But ugh." I knew the psychiatrist would put me back on lithium.

"Why the ugh?"

"I don't like being on medication. Remember the side effects?"

"If you need it, you need it. Better than losing touch with reality." He made his case gently. I couldn't argue with that logic. And yet, I felt pulled backward. I'd had a joyful pregnancy—my hormones aligned to the point of buoyancy.

My new psychiatrist, a forty-something who dressed impeccably in silk blouses and form-fitting merino-wool skirts, booked me in immediately. She told me postpartum depression for someone with my history needed urgent attention.

"It's nothing to be ashamed of. A lot of women get it," she said. Compared to her elegant getup, I felt super schleppy in my jeans and flannel shirt. This made me sink further into the abyss.

"Will I still be able to nurse at all?"

"No. Lithium transfers in breast milk. So, you better start weaning your baby off now. We need to get you on medication in a week." She sounded stern.

"That seems so fast. What if she has a bad reaction?"

"She'll be fine. You've nursed long enough." Sterner still.

"You sound like my husband," I said, relieved I now had a doctor's permission slip to return to work.

As the psychiatrist predicted, baby Hannah did fine being weaned. She sucked down the baby formula and started rounding out. Her thighs stippled with baby fat, and dimples appeared on her cheeks. I felt less depleted and more with it. Alternating between guilt and relief at relinquishing my bovine duties, I gathered my wits enough to start looking for a caregiver and plot my return to work.

Through my neighborhood moms' network, I found a family just a few blocks up the hill from us looking for another baby to share their caregiver expenses. I raced over to interview the Peruvian caregiver, Rosa, and to meet the other family. Rosa had an ear-to-ear smile and a palpable affection for her little charge Colin, a Gerber-baby blond-haired boy with wide blue eyes, six months Hannah's senior. Hannah would have an adorable playmate—no loneliness for her.

Rosa lifted me out of my guilt/anxiety cycle. I could go back to work part-time, reclaim my professional self, and spend time with friends and colleagues. But continuing to practice criminal law seemed untenable. Once I had a child, I couldn't go back to being immersed in the darkest side of human nature for long. As a mother, I needed light.

THE SUM OF MY SCARS

LESLIE FERGUSON

When I was in my twenties, my best friend and I went tubing down the Salt River in Tempe, Arizona. We swirled around with hundreds of others and bumped into a tube full of teenagers. One of the guys stared at my stomach and asked me if I'd been shot. He seemed genuinely impressed that I was still alive.

I wish I had told him someone tried to take me out in a dark alley and bullets were no match for my rock-hard abs. But I was a terrible liar, so I lowered my head, regarded the five pink, mottled keloids on my stomach, and told him the unimpressive truth: I had to have moles removed. "You know," I said, as I tentatively ran my fingers over each scar, "to check for skin cancer."

My body, a galaxy of freckles and moles, excites even the dullest dermatologist. And my doctor prefers me this way, carved and biopsied rather than melanoma-ed and dead, which I appreciate every time he cuts me. These aren't the only scars that tell the story of who I am and where I've been. I am flesh and bone and blood, and I've been lacerated, trimmed, sliced, excised, biopsied, sutured, sewn up, and sent home.

When I was twenty-two, I broke my foot playing basketball. In the ER, the doctor fitted me with a cast from foot to knee. Four weeks into my six-week healing period, I noticed extreme swelling and pain from ankle to groin, and by the time the doctor took me seriously, my knee was spilling out like raw dough over the rim of my cast, and my leg was fourteen days deep into a blood clot.

"It's a good thing you persisted," the doctor said. "A few more days, and you could've died."

I was an outlier—a young, healthy athlete with a rare clotting disorder that often kills its host before it can be detected. The doctor prescribed a blood thinner to keep my blood's clotting factor at a therapeutic level. Repeated blood draws over the years have taught me I have one very good vein in my left arm. All the phlebotomists love it. I haven't yet had one ask me if I'm a heroin addict, but I can see the curiosity in their eyes as they run their gloved index finger over the Tic-Tac-sized scar I've developed in the crook of my arm from all the needle jabs.

When I was twenty-six, I stared in awe at my wedding photos, zeroing in on my neck, on a prominent lump that made the front of my throat appear segmented and strange, like that of some alien creature.

I ran my fingers from chin to collarbone. The photos hadn't lied. I had a *neck* lump. Once, I saw a woman on the street with a neck goiter so large, she had to rest it on her shoulder to hold her head up. I felt sorry for her and wondered why she didn't have it removed. I refused to be that woman, so I asked a surgeon to slit my throat, and he removed my unsightly lump, along with part of my thyroid.

Afterward, the sutured line across the base of my neck, raw and tender, made me feel like an old rag doll coming apart at the seams. For more than a month after the thyroidectomy, every time I sat up, I remained hunched like a bobble-headed monster, wobbly and top-heavy as though if my neck would bust open, all the stuffing would pop out.

Over time, the wound healed into a scar, a branding that gave no meaningful, concrete details about who I was, how kind I'd been, or how much I'd bled.

In my thirties, a CT scan revealed a mass of unidentifiable containment or origin. Surgery was scheduled. I imagined the surgeon, in his sky-blue scrub cap, diving into me, becoming tiny in my waters, and like a deep-sea welder, using his tools to move obstructions, explore the anomaly, and cut, repair, and cauterize the area before rising to the surface slowly enough to avoid getting the bends.

After I'd regained consciousness, the doctor explained that there was no mass. But he did find uterine scarring throughout my intestinal region caused by endometriosis, a disorder in which tissue that normally lines the uterus grows *outside* of it.

What did it say about me that my insides were *inside out*? This was more than a reconnaissance mission—this was another battle of my body against itself.

My uterine scarring was so thick, so fibrous, it had adhered to my large intestine. So, to remove all of the scar tissue, the surgeon had to extract twelve inches of my colon, too. The diagonal scar that now begins above my belly button and extends three inches to the right is my souvenir, a signpost that reads "Nothing to See Here."

Nobody can see the inside—the decades-long war the body has fought—the cutting away and hollowing out, the removal of pieces and parts we can survive without. The body has an amazing ability to appear whole when the real story lies buried deep in the DNA.

That is where the scariest truths live, the ones that circle like storms inside my existence, where no medical doctor can reach them.

What nobody sees—and what we hope stays hidden—are the internal scars the museum-body collects. One thing that can never be cut out of me is the stubborn, invisible chaos of childhood trauma caused by my mother's paranoid schizophrenia. Even after she tried to kill me when I was six years old, I wanted to grow up to be like her. And I wanted more than anything for her invisible scars to heal her unpredictability and violence so she could love me freely without the voices in her head distorting her reality.

In the third grade, I wrote an essay claiming I would be married with two kids by the time I turned twenty-seven. When we are young, the realms of possibility lie only in what we can see and in what we are told to believe. If my teacher wanted me to fantasize about my fake future, I could pretend I would survive long enough to have a family of my own. But mostly, because of my mom, I did not want children, and as I learned more about mental illness, I considered it irresponsible and selfish to play the odds and tempt unpredictable genetic outcomes. She wrote me a letter once that she'd intended as a suicide note, and in it, she directed me not to have children. Maybe I interpreted this as her admission that she wished she'd never had me. Maybe my lack of desire to have children was subconsciously forged by her command, as if my obedience to her could convince me I was worthy of her love.

As I grew older, and safer away from my mom, the invisible war inside my body painfully raged on. I discovered I had less control over procreation than I realized. By the time I was forty-one, endometriosis had sown a garden of scars into my uterine cavity, and to quell the searing agony, my only option was to have a total hysterectomy.

"Even if you'd wanted kids," my doctor said, "you wouldn't have been able to have them." This was my body's way of saving me. My body knew my bloodline had suffered enough and didn't need anybody's permission to shut down the warehouse that would've otherwise been equipped to make babies. And that's when I began to understand how physical trauma often becomes entangled with emotional trauma.

Low over my pelvic region, the scar from the excavation of my uterus sits; it is a six-inch line over a purpled horizon separating my stomach from my bikini area. Almost a decade later, it is still numb, as if trying to make me forget what went on under there—and what had to happen to protect me from worse pain, from a future with children who would have been afflicted with my mother's terrible disease.

Because I never wanted children, I am lucky. But I don't care who you are, there is something very unsettling about raw, blatant truths. They are like a slamming door, closed for eternity, on your beating heart.

My traumas and scars are portals to my youth. They are sorrow and wisdom in—and under—my skin. Some external scars ache as if with the echoes of doctors' voices discussing how close I came to death. Some have turned whitish, rugged, and slim. Others are faded and smooth as if to remind me that time is not meant to heal all wounds, only to quiet their fire.

With each new scar, I have become more of a miracle. I know I can be cut away little by little and still remain whole. Maybe this is why scars endure: so we will never forget that we needed to be weakened and broken in order to understand how strong and capable we are. I did not inherit my mom's schizophrenia, but the memory of it— and the anxiety that comes with being the adult child of a mentally ill parent—reverberates in my body and my heart.

I am proud to have fought so many battles. My scars remind me of all the times I had to be opened so I could be *changed*. And I don't want to forget my trauma; it has made me who I am. I've said it before, and I'll say it again: my scars remind me how lucky I've been.

HOME IS THE PLACE

NANCY O'SULLIVAN

"Dad?"

Dry-lipped and open-mouthed, he exhales unevenly, through a flutter of skin and membrane. His tongue is thick and pink, coated white, and his breath is horrible. I pull back and wrap my hands around the tight curve of the bed rail.

A ceiling vent clicks as the shadow of a bird passes his window. Outside, October fires rage across the county, obscuring the sun and thickening the air. Inside, ashy light seeps through venetian blinds, across webs of capillaries, and into the transparency of my father's skin.

His roommate silently reads a Louis L'Amour western in his waterproof upholstered chair. My dad's watch and dentures and a food-stained copy of the *Wall Street Journal* lie on his bedside table. Several months ago, my father got a call, someone handed him the phone by his bed, and the caller asked if he wanted to receive the *Wall Street Journal*. Yes, he did. For years he'd read it when he'd been vice president of a bank, when he'd had a grand home with his second wife, two small kids, and a dog who loved him. Those were days before a recession, before the bank let him go, before he holed up in his motor home with the dog and drink. Before, as he described it, his wife got the devil in her eye and threw his belongings out the front door.

The scent of overcooked green beans drifts in. I uncurl my hands, drop my arms, and roll my shoulders. My visits have become shorter and shorter. They are as easy as dragging a dead weight over dry grass. My father rarely opens his eyes now, but he can. The specialist says he sees in

101

slivers, and only to the right, catching stripes of hands, bedsheets, and curtains. He seeks meaning and familiarity in each slice of face.

In his mind, though, the pictures are whole. He time-travels backward, a full participant, not just an observer. Last time I was here, he thought there were puppies under his bed. We should go quickly to the street, he said, to protect them. He sobbed for the puppy that was killed by a car right then and there in front of him. I stroked his shoulder and gathered his sadness in.

Secrets of his life are revealed when he travels this way. He can't choose. He can't hide. He can't curate his story. I learn my dad. He is easier to know in his senility. The dog was perhaps the only thing that loved him when he was six.

There was an empty cavern where his father's love and respect should have been. He deeply wanted to be a good father.

I soften toward him as we travel together. I soften toward the child in pain, toward the adult still longing for his father's acceptance, toward the young man entering parenthood with all of the longing and none of the tools.

The food cart bangs into the door frame, and my father slowly opens a crusty eyelid. I wipe the other eyelid with a damp cloth to unstick it.

"How are you, Dad?"

Shadows fill the hollow of his temple.

He dips his nose a centimeter down. "Fine," he rattles, "I'm fine." Confined to bed, unable to dress, swallow properly, or wash himself, the man tells lies. I want him to stand up and yell, "I am not fine! Make me better! Give me privacy, my dignity, my mind!"

But the last time he heartily expressed an opinion, he lunged at a nurse. She was, according to doctor's orders and nursing home protocol, trying to draw blood through his paper-thin skin. That day, I approved increasing his antidepressants and his antipsychotics back to the level they had been before the state decided each and every recipient of state aid really only needed one antidepressant and one antipsychotic drug.

He reaches his hand upward. "You," he said. "You're here."

I squeeze back.

I feed him puree of beef, puree of green beans, and puree of apple pie. I watch his face wrinkle up as if I had given him grapefruit, under-ripe persimmon, ice.

When his second marriage collapsed, my father packed up the motorhome and called on the hospitality of old friends. Just for a few days, a week, a few months, as long as he needed. My father found God and traveled from apostolic church to apostolic church, laying on hands and casting out demons. They called him brother and praised his gifts. To his sons and the women in his life, he wrote letters condemning us to each other for our wayward, unholy ways, for collecting graven images, for being possessed by the devil, for not bending properly to the will of a husband or father who was, by all rights, the head of the household, second only to God.

We had a few tense years there, my father and I. Decades, really.

But when the time came, when he had his strokes, when he officially lost his mind and most of his motor function, all four children from both his families gathered in the hospital in Middletown, Connecticut. We answered hospital staff as well as we could.

"He's had high blood pressure for years, but he trusted God to heal him," I said. The doctor paused momentarily as if he, too, were unable to speak his thoughts. My older brother answered next. "He lives with his friend, Jeff, has a room there." It was a small greenhouse on a winding road surrounded by maples and oaks. The house needed a new floor by the back door. It smelled of well-oiled tools, wood, and aging carpet.

"Is he gay?" the doctor asked.

"Certainly not!" my younger brother snapped, while the rest of us briefly considered if this were something else we didn't know about our father.

"Is he alcoholic?"

"He was," I said. He wasn't actively drinking, as far as we knew. "What made you ask?"

"He had tremors and other symptoms in the ICU," the doctor replied. Dad told us he cast out the demon of drink. He said he felt the power of God in his hand and had demonstrated how it vibrated as the holy power surged. His emerging Parkinson's diagnosis set this in a new light.

My siblings and I put protective boundaries between ourselves and our father, the intensity depending on how directly we'd stood in the fire of his anger and criticism. Our youngest sibling knew our father loved him. My sister made a good clean break. My older brother and I broke away and then stood by. We ebbed and flowed in the hope that stray moments of connection would come our way, some gentleness, respect, a moment of kindness.

In the Middletown hospital, right after his strokes, our father had taken his first swing at a nurse. He thought he was in the hospital to which his mother had been committed for nearly all of his childhood. Same city, similar name, different hospital.

When my siblings and I settled him into a nursing home in Connecticut, his church friends brought him burgers and twenty-ounce Cokes, then looked away and said goodbyes when he wet his chair. When staff called me for the fifth time to make life-altering decisions from the other side of the nation, I knew we had to bring him home to California. We'd taken in people before—a mom and a son in a tough situation, a homeless man who came for Thanksgiving and stayed six months, a Chilean student, friends of friends who needed a place to overnight—how could we not take in my father? Even if that meant in a nursing home?

You do that for family, right? You turn the car back on the road to the nursing home after you have veered off to buy yourself a coffee—a big one with chocolate and whipped cream, even though it is afternoon, you are trying to lose weight, and it's too expensive. You drive out of the parking lot and by the power of concentration, you do not stop at the grocers or bakery for things he may or may not appreciate. You drive to the nursing home even though your gut is lashed to your sternum so you are only breathing at the top of your lungs, your shoulder blades feel bound to all six fused bones of your skull, and your neck no longer bends as it should.

You go. You wait. You feed him and listen to whatever comes out of his mouth. You time travel back with him. You hold him when tears stream down his hollowed cheeks and he quotes Robert Frost—

"Home is the place where, when you have to go there, they have to take you in."

Tomorrow, I have a meeting with the newly gathered hospice team. They offer help. To Dad and to me. They know what loss looks like. I am afraid they will pull the sinews that bind before I am ready, and I will come apart in front of them. Like my dad, I prefer my sorrows buried, private, silent. When he goes, we are done. We will have said all that we will say to each other. Understood all that we will understand. Forgiven all that we can.

THE SWEETEST SONG

THOMAS COURTNEY

My mother cussed like a sailor when I was a kid. The only real issue with it was that she was almost entirely deaf. Although she had learned to speak like a hearing person, she never quite got the gist of what made cussing so special.

"Poopie poop doopy poopy shit fuck poopy doo!!!!"

It went a little something like that. I remember that many things had a "doo" at the end. Others had a "loo." Her brother was *Bobalu*. My Nana became *Nanalu*. My name was *Chamas,* and sometimes *Tomalu.* And, of course, that meant that my mom, Sandy, became *Sandralu.*

Every morning when she woke up, the first sounds coming from her bedroom were "Beepie beepity beep beep boooooop." This was how she checked her hearing aids. It meant she was ready to roll. With the hearing aids going full steam, she'd sing Neil Diamond to herself, off-key and at a high volume, as serious as a heart attack.

I found everything about her so fascinating as a child. I mean, the woman put cheese puffs in her chocolate pudding and had statues of dachshunds next to her TV stand to honor the dearly departed.

It's strange when you are a hearing child and are left alone with a lip-reading deaf woman. Of all my childhood memories, the strongest was watching her lean down to be eye to eye with me and saying, "Tomalu, listen to me with your good ears." She would then put her soft hands on either side of my face and say, "And I will listen to you with my heart."

106

Years later, I often remember her words when I have tough days interacting with students as a teacher. After one of those tough days, I sat in my living room. My wife handed me a phone, and I saw a grave look on her ashen face. It was my dad on the line, my mom's ex-husband. My mother wasn't just born deaf; she was born with an enlarged heart. She had survived two open-heart surgeries a decade before I was born. I had been dreading a call like this for years.

Two hours later, I was by her bedside in the emergency room at Kaiser in Fontana. Her smiling face, always full of joy and silliness, was replaced by fear and heartbreaking pain. I quickly learned that my mother had spent more than twenty-four hours on her living room floor after suffering a massive stroke. Found by a neighbor, she was rushed to the hospital.

I reached for her hand lying on the bedside, and tears filled my eyes. It was limp, soft, clammy.

"The stroke hit her left side," a doctor told me. "She can use her right hand . . . we think. For now."

Somehow, someway, we made it through the next several grueling weeks. And somehow, someway, my mother pulled through. We brought her to San Diego to a skilled nursing facility so I could be near her, visit her, and care for her.

It was there I would learn what I dreaded hearing most.

"Left-hemisphere strokes hit the brain's speech center," a doctor told me, one warm San Diego afternoon. "Your mom's speech is severely affected by this traumatic event."

I stared at my mom, who was lucid, wide-eyed. She looked from family members to the doctor as if she wanted to tell us all something rather obvious. But she couldn't say a word, not then, not ever again.

One of the most painful things I have ever done was sit by my mother's side in those months. I would lift my four-year-old son into my truck, into his car seat, and take him to see his Nanalu. In those years, he never went anywhere without his Bob the Builder construction hat, Superman cape, and Peter Pan dagger, complete with a scabbard and belt. Each visit felt unreal: walking into the lobby, signing into the guest list, passing the fish tank, smelling the cafeteria food from the dining area, and hearing the beeps and the whirring machines, the sounds of throaty coughs, and murmuring TVs from dark rooms directly off the large, carpeted hall.

I remember watching my son hold his nose past the soiled linens in the wheeled laundry tubs outside the rooms and, of course, seeing my mother's one-sided smile when we entered her room, watching her raise her thin pale hand, the one that still responded to her, in the only greeting she could still give. Sometimes, we would come at the wrong time, and my mom would suffer the indignity of a nurse needing to come in to change her before our visit. I'll never forget how the staff seemed excited to have her ready for us. On Sundays, they'd dress her in her Chargers jersey for our visit. Always we would walk in, and my son and I would hold her good hand, and he'd tell his *Nanalu* that he loved her. And I would tell *Sandralu,* my mother, that I loved her. And she would mumble back what she could, but not in her accent or anything we ever understood.

In those days, we took what we could get. Months later, I sat with her, telling her that she shouldn't lose hope, that anything could happen that might give her back some semblance of a life. As I held her hand, I remembered being with her in our backyard, bringing her bright-yellow musty dandelions, telling her, "I love you, Mommy." She wouldn't say it back until I put the flower in the palm of her hand and I pulled her chin to look at me so that she could read my lips as I said, "I love you, Mommy," and then she would always answer. She would say in her sweetly accented voice, "I ruv you too, Tomalu."

But now, she was simply silent. Her words had been taken from her mouth. For six months, all I wanted was to hear her tell me something. *Anything.*

Then, one day, I visited my mother in the afternoon on a short day at work. There by her side, was a speech therapist working with her on visual aids. I had never seen the speech therapist time, as I could only visit in the evenings after work. I could tell that there was something special going on in the way my mother was communicating with the pictures. She was pointing to things and making choices about what kind of dessert she wanted, which, of course, was chocolate pudding. For the first time since her stroke, I saw a spark.

The therapist turned to me, smiling. "Your mom is a special lady."

"I miss her voice," I told the therapist.

"I heard she likes Neil Diamond?"

"She sure does," I smirked. "She's got the massive hots for him. When I was a kid, I used to have to write down all his songs for her. Then she'd read my lips, and we'd both sing off-key together."

"Would you like to sing with her today?"

"I . . . uh . . . well . . . yeah," I stuttered, giving the therapist a kind smile. The truth was I hadn't lost hope; I just didn't know what to do with it anymore.

"Many stroke patients who have lost speech can do a few things you wouldn't expect," she explained. "We think it has something to do with the hemispheres where certain things reside in the brain. Pick a song," she said.

I didn't know what to say. Finally, I stammered out one of her favorites. "Song Sung Blue"?

She placed her phone, set to the song, on the bed next to my mother, and my mom, half-smiling, reached for my hand with her good one. I took it gently, held it in mine, and began singing along with Neil Diamond in front of this stranger. My mother watched my lips, and then the miracle happened.

She began to sing.

It was magic, like a memory that had died and had been struck by lightning in a mad scientist's lab. My mother sang along with me in her perfect, beautifully accented voice. My mother's joy and vivaciousness had returned for a timeless moment, and so had her beautiful soul. It had been there the whole time. I just had to listen to her with my good ears—and a little of her heart, too.

MY ONLY RELIGIOUS EXPERIENCE

VALERIE E. LOOPER

We stood in the living room with my packed bags and Davey, my little son, on the floor playing with his favorite toy car. I was twenty-seven, and my son was only one. Bill looked at me, questioning.

"I am leaving you," I said.

"You're not. You're not."

I had known that the marriage was a mistake within the first six months, and I had been trying diligently to work things out with Bill until I found out I was pregnant. That day, it hit me that I did not have it in me to raise both a husband and a child. While I thought we were making plans for the future, he would work until he qualified for welfare, then lose his job.

The last straw was when I took Davey, flush with fever, to the doctor and did not have money for amoxicillin. After that, I made my own plans, and today, I had packed and would go home to tell my parents I had left him.

Bill came back earlier than I expected, and when he heard me utter the words, "I'm leaving you," he promptly left the room and returned with the gun.

A bolt of electricity ran through my bones. I sank down on the couch, feeling every bit of the difference between my five-foot-nothing, 95-pound frame and his at six foot two, 220 pounds. If it came to it, fighting was not an option.

Some part of me was in shock, but another part almost expected this. He had acquired the gun a few months back. He claimed it was a "ladies' gun" that he bought for my defense after a business near his workplace had been robbed and a secretary pistol-whipped. He also took lessons and visited the practice range without me. The gun itself was a .44, far too large for a purse.

This was no ladies' gun.

Another thing that unsettled me was the way he always messed around under the hood of my car. He claimed he was a car guy, and I knew those squealing brakes needed to be fixed, but somehow, he never managed to put on new pads. I suspected he was trying to find a way for me to have an accident.

When I saw the gun, time slowed to a stop.

I knew all I had to do was press him a little bit the wrong way, and he would explode and kill one or both of us.

This may be where and when it gets decided, I thought. *If I can get myself and Davey out of here today, we all live. I don't want any of us to die, but I may die today.* My chest tightened, and I thought, *Not my baby!*

Though I was a scientist, the nuns in Catholic school taught me what to do when facing death. I tossed off a quick prayer: *"Father, into Your hands I commend my spirit."*

At that moment, I heard a voice as clear as another person in the room.

It said, *"Wait."*

With that, I felt like I had been plunged underwater. In that world, my thoughts always slowed a bit, as if my busy mind stopped throwing off trivia. I felt surrounded by weight and could see with great clarity.

Yet I could still hear Bill talking. He settled on the chair opposite me with the gun carelessly in his lap and said, "I am not going to let you leave me."

I kept still, waiting and watching. *You might kill me*, I thought, *but you will have to look me in the eye to do it.*

"Divorce means failure," Bill said. "Everyone will know."

With cinematic clarity, I saw us in the room, and separately, clips of us with the beer and comic books, the endless mess in the checkbook, the $400 custom-made boots for Dungeons & Dragons play, the mortgage payments that had been diverted to pay for the new Mazda RX-7, the money borrowed from his parents. *Everyone already knows.*

He pointed that gun at my little son playing on the floor and said, "Problem."

He pointed that gun at me and said, "Problem." I waited.

And then he pointed the gun at his own head and said, "Problem."

Then, I knew what to do and said, "You know you don't want to do that."

His mood broke for a moment, and Bill dropped his head. "Everything I do turns to shit. I am a total failure."

I let him talk, whine, cry. He started whipping himself up again, now angry. "I am doomed."

Then, for some reason, at that moment, I told him the biggest lie I had ever told in my life.

"My daddy expects to see me in three hours." We lived in Houston, and it would take a little under three hours for me to drive home. A preliminary call was an obvious step I should have taken, but I didn't.

I was poorly prepared to lie, too, but that one slipped out of my mouth as smooth and easy as if it had been commonplace truth.

Bill said, "You bitch," and started to cry.

"Give me the gun," I said. He refused but gave me the bullets from the gun instead and then went to put the gun away right next to the rest of the bullets.

When I finally left—and I can't quite remember how—I picked up the gun and bullets. Then I put them in my car.

***

I walked out the door and promptly tucked that experience away for fifteen years until I was—of all places—at an HIV conference in Budapest. The gathering of world-class minds was exhilarating, intense, and a flood of ideas. I'm not sure how we got to the subject of the supernatural as a lunchtime parlor game with a side of espresso. The question on the table: have you ever had a religious experience?

These scientists were the best of the best, but spirituality and religion were not something we talked about.

Nevertheless, the study of creation can sometimes lead to a sense of awe among scientists. Many of them wrestle with the notion that, regardless of the lack of proof, this universe has the fingerprints of Something all over it.

I drew a blank while one researcher after another casually related ordinary experiences of the transcendent.

When it came to my turn, I said, "I don't think I've ever had a religious experience."

But it was Peter, the ringleader with the amazing hazel eyes and fashionable glasses, who saw my wheels had been turning and said, "You've been thinking about something. What was it?"

And then, it tumbled out. Suddenly, I was back in my living room with my then-husband, Bill, and my one-year-old son, and I told it all.

"I said, 'Father, into your hands I commend my spirit,' and all I got was 'Wait.' If it was a religious experience, it was not very satisfying. All I got was one word. What kind of religious experience is that?"

Marta, a researcher with gentle, understanding eyes, reached out to me. "The number of words of Divine guidance does not matter if the guidance was sufficient. You say you and your son got away safe, so it must have been enough."

Years of pent-up angst over that moment seemed to be washed away. I was surprised at how much comfort I took from hearing someone else say that.

As I walked back to my hotel for the night, I thought back on that fateful day.

That was the day I won the whole world for me, Davey, my future children, and even Bill and his subsequent children. I was changed, too.

From that day forward, I have had a firm and serene conviction that I have everything I need. I've traveled far, through storms and heart-break since then, but I have never become untethered. I left my soul in His hands and have never taken it back.

DFQ

CAROLINE GILMAN

You may wonder what I, someone who was allergic to smoke, was doing hanging out nightly in a cigar shop. I had moved to Hollywood in 2013 after accepting a new job. The city itself was in stark contrast with the friendly beach town I had left; the adjustment wasn't easy. I was thirty-four, newly single, and felt like an unwelcome stranger. At coffee shops, earbuds choked out the chance for conversations. It seemed everyone thought they were a somebody and, apparently, had time for nobody. Making friends was challenging, and dating seemed impossible.

I welcomed the company of my boxing coach, Andrew. After our workout, we decided to grab a pizza at a place by my house.

"Wanna continue to hang while I grab a stick?" he asked, pointing to the cigar shop next door.

"Sounds good," I responded, nervous to enter the smoke-filled room but not ready to relinquish the companionship I missed so dearly.

As smoky as the cigar shop was, I found it refreshing. I was the only female, but I have always had male friends, so this didn't bother me. The conversations were stimulating. We discussed Malcolm Gladwell's *Outliers* and argued over what characteristics make a strong president. I befriended the shop owner and his sidekick, Adam, and soon found myself back at the shop, again and again, drinking wine while the men smoked.

Adam was a character. Overweight, loud, funny, and loved to be the center of attention. The type of guy I best tolerated in small doses. He would tell extravagant stories like the time in his teens when he circled a yacht on a Jet Ski in Monte Carlo, trying to flirt with a girl, and had guns drawn on him because, apparently, she was Spanish royalty. My eyes would involuntarily roll, listening to those outlandish tales.

I thought he was full of crap most of the time, funny until about 1:00 a.m. when he became obnoxious. After a few glasses of wine, I became feisty, so it turned into a comedic battle of his horrible attempts to flirt versus my one-liners that had most of the guys on the floor laughing.

"You guys will either end up marrying or killing each other," one guy declared, followed by another chiming in, saying, "My money's on her killing him!" Laughter erupted.

Then one night, Adam threw down the gauntlet. "I want to do this Special Ops-type challenge, but none of my guy friends are man enough to do it with me. It's this intense endurance event where you have to carry a backpack full of bricks on this overnight mission."

"You couldn't pay me enough money to do something like that," one guy responded.

"Actually, you have to pay to do it,"—Adam laughed—"but if you complete it, you get a patch."

"A patch?" The guys laughed.

I squirmed in my seat, annoyed, listening to him rant. So, I called his bluff.

"I'm in."

He smiled as he dismissed my words, the huge stogie resting between his lips. The others looked on quietly.

"I'll do it with you; how do we sign up?" I said louder.

"You should really watch the videos first before you decide you want to do this. It's Navy SEAL-type shit."

"You should really hit the gym before *you* decide to do this," I snapped back, and a roomful of "ohs" followed.

"Duh, obviously, I'd need to train first. I couldn't do it at this weight." Finally, he was speaking the truth.

Though I doubted he would even remember this conversation in the morning, I continued. "So tomorrow—well, actually today," I said, noting how late it was. "Six a.m. then?"

He checked his watch as the rest of the shop looked on. The smile on both sides of the oversized cigar returned.

"Six it is." And just like that, challenge accepted.

To my surprise, Adam showed up for the workout on time. He gave me a printout of the challenge registration; we had three months to prepare.

We met before work to run, ruck with our weighted backpacks, or climb Runyon Canyon. In the evenings, we hit the boxing gym. We dined together, swapping kale salads for pizzas.

Outside of the shop, I discovered a different Adam. I learned that he drove eight hours to ring in the New Year every year with his parents. He loved acting and was even a third-degree blackbelt. And he was the kind of guy who always showed up. Always.

One day, I picked up one hundred pumpkins for a children's pumpkin-painting party my work was hosting. My car started to smoke, and I had to pull over. So, I called Adam. He dropped everything, packed his backseat with pumpkins, and took me to work before returning to my car to get it fixed.

Adam was a hard worker, and he didn't know it, but he was pushing me too. It was as if we were both shedding weight. For him, it was pounds; for me, it was the walls I had built to protect my heart. Within a span of three months, Adam lost ninety pounds, and I gained an unlikely boyfriend.

We showed up to the event with a backpack full of bricks at 9 p.m. at the pier in Newport Beach on a chilly January night. Adam, who was fighting a cold, assured me, "I'm okay. No matter what I say, don't let me quit."

"No problem, I'm good at ignoring you," I joked. Adam didn't laugh, the humor drowned out by the nerves. My stomach was in knots, too, though I played it cool. All of the other participants were active or ex-military; Adam and I were fish out of water. One of the guys showed off his DFQ tattoo. DFQ was the company's motto: *Don't Fucking Quit*. With shaky hands, we signed the required death waivers. *What had we gotten ourselves into?*

The cadre, a former Navy SEAL, ordered us to line up, facing down the beach, our brick-filled rucks on, arms outstretched in front of us.

"Down, up!" the cadre bellowed, and we all squatted.

"Down up what?" he yelled. "This isn't Zumba. I say down, up; you say ONE, and you better be synchronized, or we start back at one."

"Yes, Cadre," the group responded.

"We're doing one hundred."

Adam looked at me with horror-filled eyes. He hated squats, and we were about to do one hundred of them.

After the squats, we partnered up and took turns dragging each other down the sand from one lifeguard tower to the next. With Adam yelling, "Babe!" every few seconds, it became apparent that Adam and I were together. Lucky me—this meant that when we paired up, it was me dragging still-far-too-heavy Adam with my measly five-foot-two frame.

"Arms out, let's go, squats, call 'em out. NINETY." I cringed, noticing the pattern.

The color drained from Adam's cheeks.

"Down up, ONE." *This is intense.*

"Down up, TWO." *How are we going to make twelve-plus hours of this?*

"Down up. THREE." *DFQ, Caroline, DFQ.*

"That's not a squat. You look like you're bobbing for apples," the cadre yelled, checking on Adam with his flashlight. I was certain that he was about to be medically dropped, but the cadre allowed him to continue.

As we pressed on, our joints throbbed, our hands swelled from dehydration, our shoulders ached where the straps of our heavy rucks dug in, and perhaps the worst pain was the sand chafing our skin raw. Several times Adam suggested we quit, but determined to hold up my end of the promise, I ignored him, and we pressed on.

We were told our final mission was a seven-and-a-half-mile ruck to the next pier. Any time the cadre blew a whistle, we had to dive into the sand as if a bomb was coming, and then get up and run on the second whistle. Hope returned to Adam's eyes at the thought of the end coming.

"Our cars are back at the other pier; there's no way we're done," I blurted.

Adam looked at me as if I had given him catastrophic news. "He said we'd be done."

"Wow, you guys finally completed a successful mission," the cadre chimed as we finally reached the pier. "So, we'll go back the easy way. Just rucking, no whistles." The group moaned.

"Told ya," I chimed.

"Eff that," Adam snapped, "I'm done. I'm calling an effing Uber!"

"I want the *fucking* patch," I bellowed, as if a monster possessed me. I wasn't quitting. I knew we could make it across that finish line, together.

The silent ruck back felt like an eternity. In the end, we did 1,290 squats, rucked over twenty-two miles, and survived over fifteen hours of physical challenges. The truth is, we could have kept going.

As for Adam and me, our mission together extended beyond the endurance challenge. In fact, DFQ became an unofficial wedding vow, and we are still going strong today, five years of marriage and a three-year-old daughter later.

IN THESE EYES

VINCENTIA SCHROETER

The pain feels like it's ripping through my left side. I am trying to keep from fainting. I think my husband is talking to me, but I can't tell. My skin is cold and clammy when I feel another sharp sonic boom of pain. I feel a wave of nausea, my head swims sideways, and I feel like I am going to pass out. I lean across the hospital cafeteria table and say, "Go get me a wheelchair." My husband Steve drops his sandwich and runs off to find one.

Sweat pours while he is gone, and I weakly look around the dining room. I can barely keep my head up, but I am desperate. As a man walks past my table, I whisper, "Please get me a doctor." He keeps walking and does not hear me. A second man walks by. I muster a louder voice and say, "I need a doctor." His eyes widen as he tells me, "I am going to the doctors' lounge." He runs to a door at the back of the room, opens it, and says, "This lady needs a doctor."

Two white coats come rushing toward me. One is the radiologist who had diagnosed my ectopic pregnancy just a few hours earlier at the ultrasound. I hear him say, "I'm in charge," just as Steve rushes in with a wheelchair.

Within seconds, I am placed in the chair and rushed down a hospital corridor. Every twist and turn hurts my belly like I am riding a bucking bronco. My remaining fallopian tube has burst, and I am bleeding internally. My baby was growing in the tube and couldn't make it to the uterus. My heart is sinking. I know that my baby will die and that I may bleed to death. I can barely breathe.

The last bump to get into the elevator jars my insides. From the elevator, I get wheeled to a room on the fourth floor. Nurse Tammy sets up an IV to jam fluids into me for emergency surgery. I can't stop shivering. Now, my body has shooting pains going up all the way to my breasts. Dr. O'Patry had warned me earlier, "If your tube ruptures, your body will fill with blood." Soon, my shoulders feel like needles are stabbing them from the inside. Steve's eyes are as scared as mine. But he is my ground. He gently says, "Can you focus on just this next breath? I am going to count breaths with you. Here we go . . ." I feel like I have been lying in a tub of ice cubes for an eternity.

A somber team in green moves in quickly. Urgent hands snap on green gloves and attach masks, I feel poking and prodding, and I smell latex and rubbing alcohol. These green-masked faces do not look into my eyes or talk to me, so I worry they won't care about me. A wave of alertness pulls me up from my shivering. I grab Steve's arm and tell him, "Tell them I need to know what is going on." Steve turns to the anesthesiologist and nurses. "You need to walk her through this and reassure her." They nod. He looks at me warmly, and my anxiety goes down as they wheel me away. I melt into the bed and surrender as we roll down to the operating room. My life is in the doctor's hands; there is nothing I can do. They will save me or not.

I awake in the recovery room and doze off and on, trying to avoid any emotions that threaten to pop up. At seven thirty the following day, my surgeon wakes me up. I feel sleepy as he checks my lungs. I ask, "How long was the operation?" He answers, "Thirty minutes." He moves to the side of the bed and looks at me seriously. "I tried to save the tube, but it was bleeding profusely, and it was impossible to save."

He had a faraway look for a minute, then came back. "I wanted to cut a wedge that could be put together later, but I couldn't. I had to cut across the fimbria." He smiled gently to soften the bad news, but all I wanted to do was roll into a cave so I could be alone in my grief forever.

I woke up after a nap feeling sad and wrote:

It's over.

I'll never be like my mother

Smiling serenely in a new

Peignoir, peeking out of her

Hospital bed window from the second floor

With a new baby in her arms

Waving to her family on the grass below.

I've carried this image of my mother and me for a long time.

Tonight I realize it will never be me.

I don't quite know who I am as a woman

anymore.

***

That evening, Steve visits after work and plops down in the chair next to me in my hospital room. He says, "I feel depressed and pissy. I fantasized about running people off the road as I drove to the hospital." I was surprised, as he is usually so even-tempered.

As we walk through hospital hallways together, I look at his face, and it pains me that he's so vulnerable. Maybe losing two babies has made us lose our protective shell, that serene sense of immunity that we had as a youngish couple.

One year later, I open my eyes after a restless night of anxious anticipation. I am so high with excitement that I need to scrape myself off the ceiling, so I can put on the pink summer dress and white pearls I have picked out for the occasion. Steve and I fly downtown, jump out of the car and race up the stairs to the placement office.

I whisper to Steve, "I don't want to move. It would be rude. They will come toward us, right?" We stand frozen on our marks, facing a white wood door, while Sister Barbara and the social worker stand behind us and to the right. The door opens.

In walks a teary nineteen-year-old blond woman in a cream-colored wool skirt and pink cashmere sweater. She dabs her red eyes with a crumpled tissue. She is holding a sleeping dark-haired bundle. Her thin, brown-haired boyfriend keeps his eyes on her, and with one arm around her shoulder, whispers words of comfort. My arms are glued to my side, but my heart is tingling with hope.

Kristy tenderly holds her sleeping baby bundled in a pink blanket as tears fill her eyes. She looks at me, and my eyes fill with love. She is about to give away a part of her heart that will never feel whole. She is about to give another mother a part of her heart that was always missing. Kristy moves closer to me until we stand shoulder to shoulder. She looks up from her baby, and her lips quiver as she asks, "So, you cannot really have a child of your own, right?" I feel the urge to drop my head in old sorrow, picturing my dark, empty womb. But I keep my head up and softly answer, "No, I can't."

She sighs and appears a bit more settled as she adjusts the blanket, swaddling her baby. I look at her beautiful pink and puffy-eyed face, and my shaky heart fills with gratitude for the gift of life she is about to give me. Kristy hands me the baby, and I am overwhelmed with joy, like everything in the world just fell into place. Soon, it will be time for the birth parents to leave. I hand the sleeping baby back to Kristy, and Steve and I sit.

She and Don walk to the furthest corner of the room. They huddle, bow their heads, and whisper their goodbyes to their birth child. It seems too private to watch, so I turn away. When they return, we all stand up. The birth father takes the baby and hands her to Steve. He gently tells her, "This is your father." At that moment, the baby, who had slept through everything, opens her eyes for the first time and looks at Steve. Steve gasps and tears up while staring at his new daughter. She has stunning blue eyes against fair skin and soft dark hair.

The second she opens her eyes, her presence fills the room. My heart dives into the bright blue swirl of those eyes, and I want to swim here forever. I see a fragile yet powerful and whole person. Like the whole meaning of my life is in these eyes. I feel a soaring new love and a touch of fear, and I am deeply humbled by the miracle that God is granting me at this moment.

ABOUT THE EDITORS

MARNI FREEDMAN

Marni Freedman is a screenwriter, playwright, award-winning author, writing coach, and co-founder and director of programming for the San Diego Writers Festival. Marni leads the Memoir Certificate Program for San Diego Writers, Ink, is the executive producer of the International Memoir Writers Association's theatrical Memoir Showcase, and co-edits *Shaking the Tree: brazen. short. memoir.* You can find Marni at MarniFreedman.com, a hub to help writers find their authentic voice.

TRACY J. JONES

Tracy J. Jones is a professional content writer, developmental editor, and writing coach. She is the co-producer, head judge, writing coach, and co-director of the San Diego Memoir Showcase. She co-edits the award-winning San Diego Memoir Showcase anthology, *Shaking the Tree: Brazen. Short. Memoir.* The fifth volume of *Shaking the Tree* will be published in January 2024. She is a co-instructor for the year-long Memoir Certificate program at San Diego Writers, Ink, and runs three writing groups. She is the President and a founding board member of the International Memoir Writers Association. Tracy is the Warwick's + San Diego Writers Festival Book Club interviewer. She can be reached at tjjones1@gmail.com.

SPECIAL THANKS

Jeniffer Thompson, and her team at Monkey C Media, for our beautiful cover and overall design. Erin Willard for copy-editing the manuscript. The entire International Memoir Writers Association for supporting this project and the San Diego Writers Festival. The IMWA board: Marni Freedman, Tracy J. Jones, Jeniffer Thompson, Caroline Gilman, Michelle Balacek, Anastasia Zadeik, Janet Hafner, Leslie Ferguson, Jocelyn Hough, and Jane Muschenetz. An additional thanks to all of our donors and angel supporters who have allowed these stories to be shared with our larger memoir community.

ARE YOU A MEMOIRIST?

The International Memoir Writers Association is a community of writers committed to the art and craft of memoir writing. Our purpose is to create a community of inspired, informed, and nurtured memoirists. We host monthly member meetings online and in person with speakers who educate our writers in both the craft and business of memoir writing, present an annual Memoir Showcase where five-page pieces are professionally performed on stage (and published in this annual Anthology), and support the San Diego Writers Festival. Writers of all levels and from all locations are welcome and encouraged to join us to help build their own writing community.

Join Our Community!

InternationalMemoirWriters.org
Facebook: www.facebook.com/groups/sdmemoirwriters
X: @SD_MWA
Instagram: @sdmwa

Also check out:
SanDiegoWritersFestival.com
join our **Book Club**
listen to our **Podcast (The Premise)**
take advantage of our **Educational Programs**